Military Certificates
of
Georgia
- 1776-1800 -

MILITARY CERTIFICATES OF GEORGIA 1776-1800

on file in the

SURVEYOR GENERAL DEPARTMENT

MARION R. HEMPERLEY

Southern Historical Press, Inc.
Greenville, South Carolina

This volume was reproduced
from a personal copy located in
the Publishers private library

All rights reserved. No part of this publication may be reproduced,
stored in a retrieval system, transmitted in any form, posted
on the web in any form or by any means without the
prior written permission of the publisher.

Please direct all correspondence and book orders to:
SOUTHERN HISTORICAL PRESS, Inc.
1071 Park West Blvd.
Greenville, SC 29611

Copyright 1983 by:

New material Copyright 2025:
 Southern Historical Press, Inc.
ISBN #978-1-63914-685-7
Printed in the United States of America

Dedicated in Memory of:

Marion R. Hemperly, Alex M. Hitz, Elizabeth Fitzpatrick John, Beatrice "Bebe" Lang and in gratitude to Janice Gayle Blake, Margaret A. Johnson and Ingrid Shields

FINDING THE MISSING GEORGIA REVOLUTIONARY WAR BOUNTY LAND CERTIFICATES

By Robert S. Davis

In addition to specific grants of land and plantations as rewards to various Revolutionary War personages, the State of Georgia offered free land to persons who had served in the state's military, refugees from the state who served in the military in other places, deserters from the British forces; and citizens who spent the last eleven months of the war in Georgia not participating in mayhem and robbery.

More than two-thirds of the bounty land certificates went to the citizens. Marion R. Hemperley did not include the citizen certificates in his book *Military Certificates of Georgia, 1776-1800* (Atlanta, 1982).

Many of the soldiers came from out of state. The Georgia State Minutemen, except for the officers, were recruited in South Carolina. Georgia's Continental troops were recruited by Georgia officers from men in North Carolina, Virginia, and elsewhere. For the history of these soldiers, see Gordon Burns Smith, *Morningstars of Liberty*, 2 vols. (Milledgeville, GA, 2006).

Because of so many fraudulent lists of persons who had supposedly sold their certificates, the state of Georgia ended this system in 1786. For the details on this process, see Alex M. Hitz, "Georgia Bounty Land Grants," *Georgia Historical Quarterly* 38 (December 1954): 337-48; and Farris W. Cadle, *Georgia Land Surveying History and Law* (Athens. GA, 1991), 73-74, 79, 82, 162.

Registers of the bounty land certificates are published as Mary B. Warren and Nichole M. O'Kelley, comps., *Georgia's Revolutionary War Bounty Land Records, 1783-1785* (Athens, GA, 1992).

FINDING A GEORGIA REVOLUTIONARY WAR BOUNTY CERTIFICATES

The certificates for bounty land took many travels before being dumped in the basement of the state capital building in Atlanta. Persons such as Telamon Cuyler took some papers that had Lyman Hall's signature as his being a signer of the Declaration of Independence made his autograph highly marketable. The capital building also suffered fire and the janitor would use loose papers in the basement to start the furnaces.

Below are places where bounty land certificates or information from them has turned up. For the bounty land certificates issued by nine states for Revolutionary War service see Lloyd DeWitt Bockstruck, *Revolutionary War Bounty Land Grants Awarded by State Governments* (Baltimore, MD, 1996).

GEORGIA ARCHIVES, MORROW

Genealogist James LeConte abstracted the certificates he found in the basement and those certificates are published in Lucian Lamar Knight, comp., Georgia's *Roster of the American Revolution* (Atlanta, 1920), 17-19, 20-192. A list of the bounty certificates but with no indication of why individual certificates were given appears in George Gillman Smith, *The Story of Georgia and the Georgia People*, 2nd edition (Macon, 1901), 630-644.

What survives of those certificates are found today in the Georgia Archives in Morrow, chiefly in the Loose Headright and Bounty Grant Papers. The Loose Headright and Bounty land Grant files and the File II files have been digitized on the Georgia Archives' free site Virtual Vault. Those files include the certificates for citizens.

The digitized files above, are only indexed by file heading, not by every name. Just doing a basic search, for example, does not turn up the list of land warrants in Burke County File II that list: William Lord (citizen), July 5, 1784; John Sebert (citizen). August 2, 1784; Fielding Freyer (?), September 6, 1784; Theodorich Goodwyn (?), November 1, 1784; Philip Jones (?), November 1, 1784; Luther Hallwell (?), March 7, 1785; Thos. Ford Sr. (?), August 1, 1785; William Patterson for heirs of James Wright (refugee), September 5, 1785; Eliazor Lewis (?), November 7, 1785; Philamon Sapp (refugee), November 7, 1785; William Lewis, Sr.(citizen), November 7, 1785; William Lewis Jr. (citizen), November 7, 1785; William Moore (refugee), December 20, 1785; George Seigar (refugee), January 2, 1786; and John Linn (citizen), March 6, 1786. The file for Peter Carnes shows that he bought the certificates from Georgia Continental soldiers: Thos. Beatty, Jno. Young, Andrew Barns, Wm. Cater, and Thomas Hall.

One way to search these files for persons not indexed in the Virtual Vault is to check to see if their name appears in *The Early Settlers of Georgia: List of File Headings of Loose Headright and Bounty Land Grant Files in the Georgia Department of Archives and History* (Milledgeville, GA, 1997) as referring you to another file, one where they are mentioned.

Other certificates are scattered about the Georgia Archives in various collections and other sources. Many bounty land certificates are mentioned in the Wilkes County land court minute books: originals, on microfilm, and published in Grace G. Davidson, *Early Records of Georgia Wilkes County* 2 vols. (Macon, GA, 1932) and presumably in the land court minute books for other counties.

Colonial Georgia Mixed Bond Book DDD (1792-1813), also has, on p. 129, a deposition of Brigadier General Samuel Elbert, August 18, 1785, testifying to men who served in the American Revolution in the 2nd Georgia Continental Battalion and for whom they are entitled military bounty land: Sergeants John Rivers, Lewis Holloway, and Lewis Clifton; and private soldiers John Dillard, John Jordan, Littleton Williamson, Joshua Moss, John Rivers, Hardy Bass, and Thomas Bass; Brittain Brantley, Timothy Simeon, William Vaughn, Lot Boyce, and Charles Clifton were killed; Meredith Tanner served until he was discharged for "bodily infirmity."

HARGRETT RARE BOOK AND MANUSCRIPT LIBRARY, UNIVERSITY OF GEORGIA

Original certificates are found today in the Telamon Cuyler Collection, Mss1170, Series 1, Historical Manuscripts.

Box 36, folder 20, James White of Richmond County, Georgia Continental soldier. No date.

Box 36, folder 21 John McDuff, citizen. No date.

Box 36, folder 34 William Hamilton, Minuteman. No date.

Box 39 folder 64, Petition of William Jones, formerly of South Carolina, certified by Caleb Howell of Effingham County of service in Florida expedition. No Date.

Box 40 folder 26 Job Pray of Savannah, mariner, 1776 until taking of Savannah in 1778. Certificate dated May 5, 1785.

Box 61 folder 9 William Cureton, lieutenant in the Minutemen. No date.

Box 62 folder 14 James Houston, soldier in the Minutemen. No date.

Box 69 folder 12 James Hall, Minuteman. March 15, 1785.

Box 69 folder 12 Joseph Robinson, Minutemen. No date.

For other bounty land certificates in the Cuyler collection in Box 62 see Robert S. Davis, *Georgia Citizens & soldiers of the American Revolution* (Easley, SC, 1979), 102-107 and "Some Miscellaneous Records of Georgia Patriots and Tories," *Georgia Genealogical Society Quarterly* 55 (summer 2019): 131-38.

Telamon Cuyler Collection, Mss1170, Series 5 Writings, Notes, and Photographs, 1904-1910, Box 172, Hargrett Rare Book and Manuscript Collection, University of Georgia Libraries, Athens. Folder 3 includes a photocopy of two Georgia Revolutionary War service bounty land certificates: Caleb Johnson as a soldier in the battalion of Lt. Col. Jno. Stewart and for 1,000 acres for Colo. William Candler as a refugee certified by Elijah Clark, colonel, February 20, 1784.

The Continental Congress Collection, 1773-1798, Mss3315, includes the citizen's certificate of William Braswell, March 15, 1785.

The Abner Atkins Collection, Mss668, has the certificate of Abner Atkins who served under Colonel Elijah Clark.

The E. Merton Coulter Collection, Mss2018, has a land warrant for Peter Wilson, May 6, 1784. It mentions that Wilson bought the land claims of 230 acres each of Continental soldiers Edwd. Day, Edwd. Smith, John Dixon, and John Shelton.

The LeConte Genealogical Collection, Mss71, contains at least copies of some bounty land certificates included among its extensive family folders.

The Felix Hargrett Collection, Mss302, has certificates for Daniel McKief (Box 1, file 24) and Joseph Oswald, refuge (Box 3, file 69).

OTHERS

The Lyman Hall Collection, Reubenstein Library, Duke University includes the bounty land certificate for James White, a soldier of the Georgia line, September 11, 1783. This collection is on microfilm at the Georgia Archives.

The Samuel Elbert Collection, Reubenstein Library, Duke University includes the bounty certificates of British deserter Brandick Tiuce/Tince; refugee soldiers Nathaniel Baker, Joseph Burgess, James French, John Girardeau, William Goulding, William Peacock Junr., and Thomas Quarterman; Lieutenant Colonel John McIntosh; heirs of Major General Robert Howe; and citizens John Anderson, Garrett Beall, John Evans, John Green, Benjamin Hall, George Harris, Robert Harris, Thos. Hensley, Thos. Hensley Junr., David Long, William Maram, Leord. Marbury Senr., Benjamin Nison (Nixon?), Robert Parker, Edwd. Roger, Benjamin Simmons, Edward Simmons, Charles Wallis, Benjamin Winn, Benjn. Watson, and John Young. William Ford is listed as "On Bounty." These records are at the Georgia Archives in microfilm drawer 282, box 61.

The Historic Augusta Incorporated Collection, Georgia Historical Society, Savannah, Ms. 1701, has the certificate of Thomas Oswald, refugee soldier, April 23, 1784.

The Samuel Rossiter Betts Autograph Collection, Ms 603, Manuscripts and Archives, Yale University Libraries, New Haven has the bounty certificates of William Paxton, October 18, 1783, and Lieutenant Cornelius Collins, September 22, 1783, filed under Lyman Hall, the governor who authorized the certificates.

Lyman Hall certified the bounty land certificate of Captain George Handley of the Georgia Line, September 8, 1783. The location of the certificate is not now known but it is described in autograph dealer's catalog no. 12947, C11278, item 20, p. 36, American Antiquarian Society, Worcester, Massachusetts.

BOUNTY LAND RECORDS FOR OTHER MILITARY SERVICE

Georgia also gave bounty land certificates to men who served in the state's post-Revolutionary War conflict called the Oconee War (1787-1790). For the history of that conflict see Gordon Burns Smith, *History of the Georgia Militia, 1783-1860*, 4 vols. (Milledgeville, G, 2002), 1: 71-96.

Lands were never given for that service and the state bought back the certificates. See "Some Soldiers of the Oconee War," *Georgia Genealogical Society Quarterly* 26 (fall 1990): 187-88. Personal information on fifteen of these soldiers is published in *Georgia Genealogical Magazine* 32 (1969): 2217.

Many of the certificates for service in the Oconee War are in Box 62 of the Telamon Cuyler Collection, Mss 1170, Series I Historical Records, Hargrett Rare Book and Manuscript Library, University of Georgia Libraries; also see Davis, *Georgia Citizens and Soldiers*, 107. Marion Hemperley includes a list of the Oconee War certificates now in the Georgia Archives and a brief history of the Oconee War in *Military Certificates of Georgia, 1776-1800* (Atlanta, 1982), 85-89, 146-50.

The federal government promised but failed to deliver on bounty land to its veterans of the Continental Army. The claims for the federal bounty land are published in the *American State Papers*, available online as word searchable at HathiTrust: https://www.hathitrust.org; also see Davis, *A Researcher's Library of Georgia*, 1: 95-112.

The national government did better by the widows and orphans of Revolutionary War veterans in 1833 and for Virginia, in 1852, see "Abstracts of Bounty Land Book NN," *Georgia Genealogical Society Quarterly* 18 (1982): 194-200; William H. Dumont, "Some Revolutionary War Soldiers and Their Heirs," *New England Historic Genealogical Society Register* 114 (July 1960): 183-90; and Margie Brown, *Genealogical Abstracts Revolutionary War Revolutionary War Script Act of 1852* (Oakton, VA, 1990).

The United States government also gave federal lands to veterans and next of kin of veterans for wars through 1855. These bounty land grant records are in the National Archives and Records Administration in Washington, DC: https://catalog.archives.gov/id/567388.

POSSIBLY NOT BOUNTY LAND CERTIFICATES

In the early Twentieth Century, someone went through the original Georgia land grant books and wrote "bounty" over Georgia grants of 287½ each, what they presumed to be grants made on the bounty. Problem comes that many people who received bounty certificates for that or in other amounts sold their certificates to other individuals who then used the certificates to obtain land grants, therefore the land is not always granted for any service done by the person who received the land grant.

For names, see Robert S. Davis, *A Researcher's Library of Georgia*, 2 vols. (Easley, SC, 2007), 1: 163-67. A similar situation exists for the Le Conte list of so-called bounty land grants identified in Lucian Lamar Knight, comp., Georgia's *Roster of the American Revolution* (Atlanta, 1920), 198-312.

PREFACE

The certificates from which this list of some 2,000 Revolutionary and Oconee War participants was compiled were part of the process whereby individuals applied for and (in most cases) received bounty land in Georgia. In order to receive that type of grant, a person was required to present a document, sometimes called a voucher, from his former commanding officer. This paper usually contains the type of service in which that person had served and, in some instances, gives his exact unit and former rank. When the voucher (or certificate as it is usually called) was presented to the state land court, and if found valid, a formal certificate was signed and issued by the Governor. Those two types of documents comprise most of the papers from which this list was extracted. In many cases, both catagories of certificates for the same person are on file. In the following study the Revolutionary War certificates have been listed first with those for the Oconee War second. For a detailed narrative giving the inclusive dates and eligibility, see appendix.

In compiling this list for use by researchers, the author attempted to extract all pertinent historical information from each certificate. On the other hand, great care was exercised to include only those certificates which correctly indicate military service from the complete file of approximately 200,000 documents.

No complete military service records exist in Georgia for veterans of the Revolutionary and Oconee Wars but with the publication of this list it is hoped that the information contained therein will help fill that void. However, to supplement military information while using this study, one should search other sources for additional data. To facilitate research and to make this list more useful, an appendix has been included outlining the various military units of that period. This narrative was prepared by Gordon Smith of Savannah, one of the leading experts in the military history of Georgia. Mr. Smith compiled that section and graciously gave the author permission to include it in this study.

A word of caution is in order concerning the correct spelling of names. Formal education had not been introduced into the society of that period and few persons could read or write. In fact many could not spell or write their own names. When a person gave his oral oath outlining his service or joined a military unit, the clerk to whom he presented himself simply spelled the name as he thought it should be. Or he spelled it as it sounded to him. Thus, one can find many documents with a person's name spelled two or even three different ways all on the same paper according to various interpretations of clerks or governmental officials who endorsed it.

When there is more than one document for the same named person, a choice had to be made by the author to determine if it was indeed the same person or not. When a decision was made that two different persons by the same name were represented, that name (with the various branches of service) was listed more than once. Hence, the researcher using this list will note than in many instances one name will be given a number of times with a different branch of service for each. However, it should be noted that one person could have been in two or more different brances of service one after the other. Enlistments were short and sometimes a person changed from unit to unit all in a relatively short period. Again further proof is needed to determine the correct status of each listing.

At the time of publication, all certificates are physically on file in the Georgia Surveyor General Department, Archives and Records Building, 330 Capitol Avenue, Atlanta, Georgia 30334. Most of the old papers are very fragile and worn and in many cases can be read only with difficulty. Time and neglect in former years have taken their toll in the condition of those documents. At the present time all papers are filed in acid-free folders under individual names in Archives Boxes. The vault in which they are housed is temperature and humidity controlled for maximum preservation.

Appreciation is expressed to my assistant, Ingrid Shields, who has freely given her support and advice. Special thanks is given to Adrienne Gibbons for reading portions of this manuscript and list and giving her critique of them. My wife Martha assisted considerably in proofreading the manuscript and Janice Gilley is to be commended for setting the whole in type. The excellent illustrations were prepared by George Whiteley of the Georgia Archives staff. Again I wish to thank Gordon Smith for the fine appendix he prepared and allowed me to include in this study. Finally, this list could not have been compiled without the complete cooperation of the Secretary of State, Max Cleland (who is also Georgia's Surveyor General). In conclusion, it should be noted that this study has been compiled by me alone and I bear all responsibility for the accuracy therein.

Marion R. Hemperley
July 1, 1983

Abanton, Isaac	Soldier in Bn. of Minute Men
Abbett, John	Refugee
Abbott, John	Soldier
Adams, David	Soldier in Bn. of Minute Men
Adams, David	Refugee
Adams, Hugh	Soldier in Bn. of Minute Men
Adams, John	Soldier, 2nd. Ga. Bn.; served for three years
Adams, John	Soldier in Bn. of Minute Men
Adams, John	Soldier in Reg. under command of Col. Leonard Marbury
Addams, Hugh	Soldier in Bn. of Minute Men
Aderedge, Thomas	Refugee
Adkins, David	Soldier in Bn. of Minute Men
Adkins, Jese	Soldier in Bn. of Minute Men
Adkins, Solomon	Soldier in Bn. of Minute Men
Akins, John	Soldier in Bn. of Minute Men
Akridge, William	Refugee
Alexander, Adam	Surgeons First Mate, 2nd. Ga. Bn., Ga. Cont. Line
Alexander, Asa	Refugee
Alexander, Hugh	Lt. in Bn. of Minute Men
Alexander, James	Refugee
Alexander, Robert	Private in Bn. of Minute Men
Alexander, Samuel	Refugee Captain
Alexander, William	Soldier in Reg. under command of Col. Leonard Marbury
Allen, William	Soldier, 2nd. Ga. Bn.; enlisted for three years and served his time faithfully
Allison, Henry	Lt., Ga. Line; served until end of war
Allison, James	Refugee Soldier
Ambler, John	Soldier in Bn. of Minute Men
Amler, John	Soldier in Bn. of Minute Men
Ammons, Robert	Soldier in Bn. of Minute Men
Ammons, William	Private in Bn. of Minute Men commanded by Col. John Stuart; resided in South Carolina

Anderson, Alexander	Private 1st Bn. of Minute Men
Anderson, Bartley	Refugee, 1st Bn., Richmond County Militia
Anderson, Edmund	Soldier, 2nd. Ga. Bn.; served for three years
Anderson, Elisha	Refugee
Anderson, Henry	Soldier in Bn. of Minute Men
Anderson, Hugh	Soldier in Bn. of Minute Men
Anderson, James	Soldier in Reg. under command of Col. Leonard Marbury
Anderson, James	Lt. in Bn. of Minute Men
Anderson, Joseph	Refugee in North Carolina
Anderson, Peter	Soldier in Bn. of Minute Men
Anderson, Richard	Soldier in Reg. under command of Leonard Marbury
Anderson, Simmer	Soldier in Bn. of Minute Men
Anderson, William	Soldier, 3rd. Ga. Bn.; served for three years
Anderson, William	Soldier in Bn. of Minute Men
Andrew, Benjamin Jr.	Refugee
Anglin, David	Soldier in Bn. of Minute Men
Anglin, Henry	Soldier in Bn. of Minute Men
Anglin, William	Soldier in Bn. of Minute Men
Ansley, Thomas Jr.	Refugee
Ansley, Thomas Sr.	Refugee
Apling, John	Refugee
Appling, Daniel	Refugee
Appling, John	Refugee
Arnold, John	Soldier, Ga. Cont. Line
Arraday, William	Soldier in Bn. of Minute Men
Arrington, John	Soldier, Ga. Cont. Line
Ashwood, Adam	Soldier in Bn. of Minute Men
Ashworth, Adam	Soldier in Bn. of Minute Men
Ashworth, Arthur	Soldier in Bn. of Minute Men
Ashworth, Arthur	Soldier in Bn. of Minute Men
Ashworth, Benjamin	Refugee
Austin, Richard	Captain in Bn. of Minute Men

Autery, Alexander Jr.	Refugee
Autery, John	Refugee Captain
Avera, Isaac	Refugee
Awtry, Alexander	Refugee Captain
Awtry, Jacob	Refugee
Awtry, John	Refugee Captian
Aycock, Richard	Refugee
Ayre, James	Soldier, Ga. Cont. Line
Ayres, Abraham	Refugee Captain; was killed in Battle of Long Cain in December 1780
Ayres, Daniel	Lt. in Bn. of Minute Men
Ayres, William	Captian in Bn. of Minute Men
Bacon, Jonathan	Refugee
Bacon, Thomas	Refugee
Baggs, John	Private in Bn. of Minute Men
Bailey, William	Refugee Lt.
Baillie, Robert	Refugee
Baine, Reuben	Soldier in Bn. of Minute Men
Baker, Artemas	Refugee
Baker, Isaac	Soldier in Bn. of Minute Men
Baker, John	Soldier in Bn. of Minute Men
Baker, John	Refugee Colonel; resides in Liberty Co., Ga.
Baker, Nathaniel	Refugee
Baker, Thomas	Refugee
Baker, Whitmarsh	Refugee
Baker, William	Refugee Major
Baker, William Jeans	Refugee
Baldwin, David	Captain in Bn. of Minute Men; was on Florida expedition
Baldwin, Mordecai	Lt. in Bn. of Minute Men
Baldwin, William	Sergeant in Bn. of Minute Men
Baldwin, Willaim	Cont. Soldier
Baley, Druland	Soldier in Bn. of Minute Men
Baley, Edmond	Soldier in Bn. of Minute Men
Baley, Isam	Soldier in Bn. of Minute Men
Baley, John	Soldier in Bn. of Minute Men

Ball, John	Private in Bn. of Minute Men
Ball, Sampson	Refugee
Ball, William	Refugee
Baly, Peter	Soldier in Bn. of Minute Men
Bane, Reuben	Common Soldier in Captain Henery Kar's Co., Stewart's 1st Bn. of Minute Men; Bane was discharged July 27, 1778
Banks, Reuben	Soldier, 2nd. Reg., Ga. Cont. Troops
Bankston, Daniel	Soldier
Barber, Chester	Soldier of the Cont. Line
Barber, George	Refugee Lt.
Barclay, Henry	Soldier, Ga. Cont. Line
Bard, John	Soldier, Cont. Reg. of Light Horse, under command of Col. Leonard Marbury
Barkelow, Richard	Refugee
Barnard, Joel	Refugee from Richmond County
Barnard, William	Refugee from Richmond County
Barnes, William	Soldier, 1st. Bn. of Minute Men
Barnett, Daniel	Refugee
Barnett, Joel	Refugee
Barnett, John	Refugee
Barnett, Mial	Refugee
Barnett, Nathan	Refugee
Barnett, Philip	Private in Bn. of Minute Men
Barnett, William	Refugee
Barnett, William	Soldier, 1st. Bn. of Minute Men
Barrer, Reuben	Soldier, 1st. Bn. of Minute Men
Barrett, Thomas	Soldier, 1st. Bn., Richmond County Militia
Barrow, Ruben	Soldier in Col. John Stewart's Bn. of Minute Men
Bartley, John	Soldier, Ga. Cont. Line
Barton, Williby	Refugee
Barton, Williby	Sergeant in Col. Samuel Jack's Bn. of Minute Men; went on Florida expedition
Basil, Owen	Soldier, Ga. Cont. Line
Bassett, George	Soldier, Ga. State Legion, commanded by

	Lt. Col. James Jackson
Baxter, Andrew	Private under Col. Elijah Clark
Beach, Peter	Soldier, Ga. Cont. Line
Beal, Archibald	Adjutant to the Refugee Reg., commanded by Col. William Candler
Beal, Jeremiah	Refugee; was killed in action
Beall, George	Soldier in Bn. of Minute Men
Beall, Henry	Soldier in Bn. of Minute Men
Beall, John	Soldier in Bn. of Minute Men
Bean, Reubin	Soldier in Bn. of Minute Men
Beanlly, Luis	Refugee
Beard, George	Refugee
Beard, John	Sergeant in Bn. of Minute Men
Beard, John	Soldier in Bn. of Minute Men
Beard, Peter	Soldier in Bn. of Minute Men
Beaty, Samuel	Private in Bn. of Minute Men
Beckman, James	Soldier, Ga. Cont. Line
Beckman, Robert	Soldier, Ga. Cont. Line
Beden, Elijah	Soldier in Bn. of Minute Men
Bedingfield, Nathaniel	Refugee
Bell, Hugh	Soldier, Ga. Cont. Line
Bell, John	Soldier in Bn. of Minute Men commanded by Col. Samuel Jack
Bell, Robert	Refugee
Bender, John	Militia Soldier in Col. William Candler's Reg.; Refugee
Bennett, John	Cont. Soldier
Bennett, Richard	Cont. Soldier
Bennett, William	Cont. Soldier
Benson, John	Refugee
Bentley, William	Soldier
Berrien, John	Major, Ga. Cont. Line
Berrihill, Alexander	Refugee
Berrihill, Samuel	Refugee
Berry, William	Soldier
Bery, Rodger	Soldier
Bevill, James	Refugee

Bevill, Paul	Refugee
Bevill, Robert	Refugee
Bickham, Abner	Refugee
Bird, John	Soldier, 1st Bn. of Minute Men
Bird, Michael	Soldier in Bn. of Minute Men
Black, Henry	Refugee
Black, James	Cont. Soldier
Black, John	Refugee
Black, William	Refugee
Blacksille, Thomas	Refugee; was a prisoner for part of the war
Blair, Samuel	Refugee
Blakey, Benjamin	Sergeant in Bn. of Minute Men
Blayer, William	Refugee
Blount, Jacob	Surgeon's Mate in the Galley Service; deceased prior to February 1784
Blount, Stephen	Refugee
Bobough, Lewis	Soldier in Ga. State Legion Infantry commanded by Lt. Col. James Jackson
Bodimas, George	Private in Bn. of Minute Men
Boles, Francis	Soldier in Bn. of Minute Men
Boling, John	Soldier, 3rd. Co., 2nd. Ga. Cont. Reg. in September, October, November, and December 1777 and January and February 1778; he was very sickly and hired a substitute, Absolom Reynolds
Bolton, Ralph	Soldier in Reg. under command of Col. Leonard Marbury
Bolton, Richard	Soldier in Reg. under command of Col. Leonard Marbury
Bonnell, John	Refugee
Booth, William	Soldier, Ga. Cont. Line
Bostick, Littleberry	Refugee
Bostick, Nathan	Refugee
Botten, Francis	Soldier in Bn. of Minute Men
Bowen, Oliver	Commodore and Commander of the Ga. Navy

Bowen, Silas	Soldier in Reg. of Dragoons
Bowin, Ephraim	Refugee
Bowin, Richard	Soldier, 1st. Bn. of Minute Men
Bowling, Robert	Refugee
Bowling, Thomas	Soldier in Reg. under command of Col. Leonard Marbury
Boyd, John	Soldier in Bn. of Minute Men
Boykin, Byus	Refugee; served in North Carolina
Boykin, Francis	Refugee
Braddock, David	Served on board the Galleys
Braddock, John	Refugee Captain
Bradley, Michael	Soldier in the 4th. Ga. Reg.; enlisted in July 1777; died in the service at Savannah; left one son, Abram
Bradley, Richard	Refugee
Bradley, Richard	Private for three years on board the Galleys
Bradley, William	Refugee
Bradley, William Jr.	Soldier in Bn. of Minute Men
Bradley, William Sr.	Lt. in Bn. of Minute Men
Bradshaw, Peter	Soldier in Bn. of Minute Men and Militia Soldier
Branham, Samuel	Soldier in Bn. of Minute Men
Brantly, Jeremiah	Sergeant in Col. Samuel Jack's Bn. of Minute Men; was on Florida expedition
Brasile, Ferdinand	Soldier, 1st. Bn. of Minute Men
Brasile, John	Soldier, 1st. Bn. of Minute Men
Braswell, Allen	Soldier in Bn. of Minute Men
Braswell, Frederick	Soldier in Bn. of Minute Men
Braswell, George	Soldier in Bn. of Minute Men
Braswell, James	Soldier in Bn. of Minute Men
Braswell, Joseph	Soldier in Bn. of Minute Men
Braswell, Sampson	Soldier in Bn. of Minute Men
Braswell, William	Refugee
Bratcher, John	Soldier in Bn. of Minute Men
Brazel, Samuel	Refugee
Brewer, Moses	Soldier

Brewer, William	Refugee
Bridges, James	Served "with Colonel Josiah Dunn's upon a scout, after torys, but was no lower down upon Ogeachee, Savannah side of the river, than Tripplit's Ferry . . ."
Briggs, Samuel	Refugee
Britt, Charles	Soldier in Bn. of Minute Men
Brittain, Henry	Sergeant in Bn. of Minute Men
Brooks, Roger	Soldier in Bn. of Minute Men
Broom, Thomas	Refugee
Brossard, Celerin	Was appointed a Captain in the 4th. Ga. Cont. Line, commanded by Col. John White; appointment dated June 26, 1777; he served in this capacity until the arrangement of the Ga. Line in 1782
Brown, Allen	Refugee
Brown, Andrew	Refugee
Brown, Francis	Private, 2nd. Ga. Cont. Bn.; served three years
Brown, Frederick	Soldier in Ga. State Legion, commanded by Lt. Col. James Jackson
Brown, James	Soldier, 1st. Bn. of Minute Men
Brown, John	Soldier, 2nd. Bn., Ga. Cont. Troops; served three years
Brown, John	Refugee
Brown, Thomas Jr.	Soldier
Brownen, Charles	Soldier, Ga. State Legion, commanded by Lt. Col. James Jackson
Brownson, Nathan	Deputy Purveyor, General Hospitals
Bruce, John	Soldier in Reg. under command of Col. Leonard Marbury
Bruce, Josiah	Soldier in Reg. under command of Col. Leonard Marbury
Brunson, David	Refugee
Brunson, Ebenezer	Refugee; was in service from fall of Augusta to fall of Savannah
Brunson, John	Refugee

Brunson, William	Refugee
Bruton, John	Refugee
Bryan, Reubin	Soldier in Reg. under command of Col. Leonard Marbury
Bryant, John	Lt. in Bn. of Minute Men
Bugg, Edmond	Refugee
Bugg, Jeremiah	Lt. Col. in Refugees
Bugg, Samuel	Refugee
Bugg, Sherwood	Refugee
Bullman, John	Soldier, Ga. Cont. Line
Bunker, Roger	Soldier in Reg. under command of Col. Leonard Marbury
Burch, Charles	Refugee
Burch, Edward	Refugee
Burdey, Peter	Soldier under Col. Elijah Clarke
Burgsteiner, Daniel	Refugee
Burke, James	Private, Ga. Cont. Line; deceased prior to May 1784; survived by Mary Burke
Burkes, Silas	Soldier in Bn. of Minute Men
Burks, David	Sergeant in Bn. of Minute Men and Militia Soldier
Burks, John	Captian in Bn. of Minute Men
Burks, Joseph	Soldier in Bn. of Minute Men
Burlamon, Benjamin	Refugee
Burnet, John	Refugee Captain
Burnett, Joshua	Refugee
Burnley, Samuel	Refugee
Burnsides, John	Refugee
Burt, Moody	Refugee
Burton, John	Soldier in Bn. of Minute Men
Burton, Richard	Soldier in Captain Isaac Hicks' Co., 3rd. Ga. Cont. Bn.; enlisted October 7, 1776 for three years
Burton, Thomas	Refugee
Butler, Daniel	Soldier in Lt. Col. Leonard Marbury's Reg.
Butler, Daniel	Soldier in Bn. of Minute Men

Butler, Daniel	Refugee
Butler, Daniel	Refugee and Soldier
Butler, Ford	Refugee
Butler, John	Soldier in Bn. of Minute Men
Butler, Robert	Soldier, 1st. Bn. of Minute Men
Butry, Zachariah	Private, 2nd. Ga. Cont. Bn.
Cade, Drury	Refugee
Caldwell, George	Refugee
Calk, James Jr.	Soldier, 1st. Bn. of Minute Men
Calk, James Sr.	Soldier, 1st. Bn. of Minute Men
Camp, Edmond	Soldier, Cont. Reg. of Light Horse, under command of Col. Leonard Marbury
Campbell, Alexander	Soldier in Bn. of Minute Men
Campbell, Drury	Lt. in Bn. of Minute Men
Campbell, Gilbert	Private in Bn. of Minute Men
Campbell, William	Private in Bn. of Minute Men
Candler, Henry	Refugee
Cannon, Thomas	Soldier in Bn. of Minute Men
Carden, Cornelius	Soldier in Bn. of Minute Men
Carey, Robert	Soldier in Bn. of Minute Men
Carlton, Patrick	Private in Bn. of Minute Men
Carney, Matthew	Private, 2nd. Ga. Cont. Bn.; served for three years
Carney, Onsby	Soldier in Bn. of Minute Men
Carr, Henry	Refugee
Carr, Henry	Lt. in Bn. of Minute Men
Carr, Patrick	Refugee Captain, later Major
Carsey, Stephen	Refugee
Carson, Adam	Soldier in Bn. of Minute Men
Carson, David	Soldier in Bn. of Minute Men
Carson, David	Refugee
Carson, John	Refugee
Carson, John	Soldier in Bn. of Minute Men
Carson, Joseph	Soldier in Bn. of Minute Men
Carson, Joseph	Refugee
Carson, Samuel	Refugee
Carson, Thomas Jr.	Refugee

Carson, Thomas Sr.	Soldier in Bn. of Minute Men
Carter, James	Refugee Captain and Aid-de-Camp to Col. Elijah Clarke at the time he (Carter) was slain in battle
Carter, Patirck	Soldier in Bn. of Minute Men
Cartledge, James	Refugee
Cartledge, James	Soldier in Bn. of Minute Men
Castillo, Edward	Soldier, 1st. Bn. of Minute Men
Castillo, Michael	Soldier, 1st. Bn. of Minute Men
Catching, Joseph	Refugee
Cathing, Merideth	Soldier
Cathing, Seymore	Refugee
Cato, William	Refugee
Catterat, Stephen	Soldier, 1st. Bn. of Minute Men
Cawley, Caleb	Soldier in Bn. of Minute Men
Cawley, Catlett	Soldier in Bn. of Minute Men and Militia Soldier
Cawley, Richard	Soldier in Bn. of Minute Men
Chambless, Christopher	Refugee
Chambless, Littleton	Served in the Revolution
Chandler, Abednego	Soldier in Bn. of Minute Men
Chandler, Mardacai	Private in Bn. of Minute Men
Chaney, Emanuel	Refugee
Chaney, Greenberry	Refugee
Chapman, John	Sergeant in Bn. of Minute Men
Chavos, Jeremiah	Refugee
Chessor, John	Soldier in Bn. of Minute Men
Childers, David	Private, 2nd. Bn., Ga. Cont. Troops
Childers, Thomas	Soldier, Ga. Cont. Line
Chisholm, Benjamin	Refugee
Chisolm, John	Sergeant, 2nd. Reg., Ga. Con. Troops
Chisolm, Thomas	Refugee
Clark, Benjamin	Refugee under command of Col. Elijah Clarke
Clark, Moses	Soldier in Lt. Col. John Stewart's Bn. of Minute Men
Clarke, Elijah	Refugee Colonel

Clarke, John	Private in Bn. of Minute Men
Clarke, John	Refugee Captain
Clarke, Lewis	Refugee
Clem, John	Soldier in Bn. of Minute Men
Clements, John	Refugee; served in North Carolina after the fall of Charleston
Cloud, Ezekiel	Refugee
Cloud, Jeremiah	Soldier, 4th. Co., Reg. of Horse, commanded by Lt. Col. Leonard Marbury, Commandant of the Cont. Reg. of Light Horse for the State of Ga.
Cloud, Jeremiah Jr.	Refugee
Cloud, Jeremiah Sr.	Refugee
Cloud, John	Soldier, 4th. Co., Reg. of Horse, commanded by Lt. Col. Leonard Marbury, Commandant of the Cont. Reg. of Light Horse for the State of Ga.
Cloud, John	Refugee
Cloud, Nenouh	Soldier, 4th. Co., Reg. of Horse, commanded by Lt. Col. Leonard Marbury, Commandant of the Cont. Reg. of Light Horse for the State of Ga.
Cloud, Neough	Refugee
Cock, Caleb	Refugee
Coleman, Daniel	Refugee
Coleman, Harris	Refugee
Coleman, James	Refugee
Collens, John	Soldier in Bn. of Minute Men
Collins, John	Private, 2nd. Ga. Cont. Reg.; served for three years
Collins, John	Private in Bn. of Minute Men
Collins, Stephen	Soldier, Reg. of Dragoons, Captain Scott's Troup
Colson, William	Refugee
Cone, James	Refugee in Col. William Candler's Reg.
Cone, William	Refugee
Conner, Daniel	Soldier

Conyers, John	Refugee Captain
Conyers, John Jr.	Refugee
Conyers, William	Refugee; served in South Carolina after fall of Charleston; was deceased prior to Dec. 1783
Cook, George	Soldier in Bn. of Minute Men
Cook, Isham	Captain in Cont. Line; died in the service of his country
Cooper, Anthony	Soldier in Bn. of Minute Men
Cooper, David	Soldier in Bn. of Minute Men
Cooper, Jesse	Soldier in Bn. of Minute Men
Corban, William	Soldier, Ga. Cont. Line
Cothorn, Josiah	Refugee; was killed while in the service
Cothorn, William	Refugee
Coucksy, William	Soldier in Bn. of Minute Men
Coup, Henry	Sergeant in Bn. of Minute Men
Cousins, William	Cont. Soldier
Cowan, Edward	Captain
Cowen, William	Refugee
Cox, Benjamin	Soldier in Bn. of Minute Men
Crain, Lewis	Soldier in Ga. State Legion, under command of Lt. Col. James Jackson
Crawford, David	Soldier, 2nd. Bn., Cont. Troops; enlisted for three years; died while in service
Crawford, John	Refugee
Creswell, Samuel	Refugee Surgeon
Croker, William	Private, 2nd. Cont. Reg.; served for three years
Cronberger, Christopher	Refugee; was unfortunately killed; survived by his widow, Barbara Cronberger
Crook, William	Private in Bn. of Minute Men
Crosby, William	Soldier in Bn. of Minute Men
Crudders, William	Private in Bn. of Minute Men
Culbreath, James	Refugee
Culbreath, John	Served in the Revolution
Cullards, Henry	Soldier in Bn. of Minute Men
Culpepper, Joseph Jr.	Refugee

Cunningham, James	Refugee
Cunningham, John	Refugee Major
Cunningham, John	Captain, 2nd. Ga. Cont. Bn.; served for four years
Cup, Michael	Soldier in Bn. of Minute Men
Cureton, William Jr.	Private in Bn. of Minute Men
Curl, Henry	Soldier in Bn. of Minute Men
Curl, John	Soldier in Bn. of Minute Men
Curry, Carey	Private in Bn. of Minute Men
Curry, Jacob	Soldier in Bn. of Minute Men
Curry, Nicholas	Refugee
Curry, Peter	Soldier in Bn. of Minute Men
Curry, Peter	Soldier in Bn. of Minute Men
Dabney, Austin	Refugee
Dampier, Daniel	Sergeant in Ga. Line
Daniel, Benjamin	Private, Captain Jacob Howell's Co., 1st. Bn., Ga. Cont. Troops; served for 12 months; discharged on April 20, 1777
Daniel, William	Refugee
Danielly, James	Refugee under command of Col. William Candler
Danielly, James	Refugee under command of Col. James McCay
Danielly, James	Soldier in Bn. of Minute Men
Dannelly, Daniel	Refugee Lt.
Dannelly, Daniel	"This is to certify that Mr. Daniel Dannelly was under my command in pursuit of McGirth's Party on the South Side of Ogeechee River, in February, 1782, and that Mr. Dannelly was wounded by the fire of the said party, in the left hand, and in the right shoulder, by which he hath lost the perfect use of his said left hand, and also of his right arm. Certified by me, then commanding a party of Carr's Independant Corps, and Liberty County Militia. /S/ Samuel West, Major, Liberty Coun-

	ty Militia."
Darby, Abraham	Soldier in Bn. of Minute Men
Darby, John	Soldier in Bn. of Minute Men
Darcey, Joel	Refugee
Darcey, James	Refugee
Darden, George	Refugee
Darling, Abraham	Refugee
Darling, Noble	Soldier in Bn. of Minute Men
Dasher, Christian	Refugee
Dasher, John Martin	Refugee
Davenport, Thomas	Surgeon in the 3rd. Bn., Ga. Cont. Troops, until he died in captivity at the beginning of 1780
Davenport, Thomas	Lt. in the Ga. Cont. Line until the end of the war.
David, William	Refugee
Davidson, John	Soldier, Ga. Cont. Line
Davidson, Robert	Soldier, Ga. Cont. Line
Davies, John	Refugee in North Carolina after the reduction of Charleston by the British troops
Davies, Myrick	Refugee Private; was a member of the Executive Council under Gov. Richard Howley; was killed by a party of Tories in December 1781
Davis, Absalom	Refugee and Militia Soldier
Davis, Benjamin	Refugee
Davis, Blanford	Refugee in Reg. under command of Col. William Candler
Davis, Charles	Sergeant, 7th. Co., 2nd. Bn., Cont. Line of Ga.
Davis, Chesly	Refugee
Davis, David	Soldier, Ga. State Legion, under command of Lt. Col. James Jackson; "House of Assembly, July 22, 1782. Resolved that a compleat suit of clothes, a good horse, saddle and bridle, a likely negro, and three hundred acres of land be given

to David Davis of Colo. Jackson's Corps, as a testimony of the appreciation of this house, for his faithfull services, and his discovering a conspiracy formed against the government."

Davis, Edward	Refugee Captain
Davis, Elias	Refugee
Davis, George	Soldier in Bn. of Minute Men
Davis, Hardy	Soldier in Bn. of Minute Men
Davis, Isaac	Soldier in Bn. of Minute Men
Davis, Isaac	Soldier in Reg. under command of Col. Leonard Marbury
Davis, Jacob	Soldier in Bn. of Minute Men
Davis, Jenkins	Colonel; lived in Effingham Co., Ga.
Davis, Joel	Refugee
Davis, John	Refugee
Davis, Meredith	Sergeant, 7th. Co., 2nd. Bn., Ga. Cont. Line
Davis, Robert	Soldier, Cont. Line
Davis, Samuel	Soldier, Cont. Line
Davis, Sherwood	Soldier in Bn. of Minute Men
Davis, Thomas	Soldier in Bn. of Minute Men
Davis, Vachael	Refugee under command of Col. William Candler
Davis, Ware	Soldier in Bn. of Minute Men
Davis, Willie	Refugee
Davison, Thomas	Soldier, 2nd. Ga. Bn.
Davison, William	Soldier, 2nd. Ga. Bn.
Dawson, William	Soldier, 2nd. Bn., Ga. Cont. Troops
Day, Harry	Refugee under command of Col William Candler
Day, Henry	Refugee
Day, Joseph	Captain, Ga. Line
Day, Robert Jr.	Refugee in Col. Elijah Clarke's Reg.
Day, Robert Sr.	Refugee in Col. Elijah Clarke's Reg. of Militia
Day, Stephen	Served in Revolution

Dean, Henry	Cont. Soldier
Dean, Samuel	Lighthorseman in the Cont. Reg., Light Dragoons in the State of Ga., commanded by Col. Leonard Marbury
Dean, William	Sergeant, 3rd. Bn. of Foot, commanded by Col. James Scriven
Dean, William	Sergeant in Light Dragoons in the State of Ga., commanded by Col. Leonard Marbury; served for three years; discharged Feb. 16, 1779
Dearden, George Sr.	Refugee under command of Col. Elijah Clarke
Deason, John Sr.	Enlisted in South Carolina in Minute Bn. commanded by Col. John Stewart
Deaster, Abraham	Refugee
DeClandinus, Mathew	Sergeant in Bn. of Minute Men
Delany, James	Private, 1st. Bn. of Minute Men
Deleonser, Abraham	Soldier in Bn. of Minute Men
Delk, David	Soldier in Bn. of Minute Men
Denkins, John	Soldier in Bn. of Minute Men
Dennes, Richard	Soldier in Reg. of Dragoons
Dennison, John	Soldier, Ga. Cont. Line
Dennison, William	Soldier, Ga. Cont. Line
Dentham, John	Soldier in Bn. of Minute Men
DeRoche, Abraham	Refugee
Deaveaux, Peter	Refugee Captain; "I do hereby certify that Peter Deveaux, Esquire, was appointed as Aide de Camp to the Honb'e Major General Gates on the second day of August last—at Mash's Ferry on the Peedee River—and continued to serve in that capacity during the general's command of the southern department. /S/ John Armstrong, Dty Adjutant General, Southern Department. Philadelphia, 14th. May, 1781."
Dicks, Andrew	Refugee

Dicks, David	Refugee; died shortly after leaving this state
Dickson, David	Captain in Bn. of Minute Men
Dickson, Hugh	Sergeant in Bn. of Minute Men
Dickson, Michael	Captain in Bn. of Minute Men
Dickson, Nathan	Soldier, 1st. Bn. of Minute Men
Dickson, Nathaniel	Private in Bn. of Minute Men
Dickson, William	Sergeant in Bn. of Minute Men
Dinkins, John	Soldier in Bn. of Minute Men
Dinkins, Sabry	Soldier in Bn. of Minute Men and Militia Soldier
Dix, Benjamin	Soldier in Bn. of Minute Men
Dix, David	Refugee
Dix, Peter	Soldier in Bn. of Minute Men
Dix, Randolph	Refugee
Dobey, John	Soldier in Reg. under command of Col. Leonard Marbury
Dobey, William	Soldier in Reg. under command of Col. Leonard Marbury
Dodds, George	Soldier in Reg. under command of Col. Leonard Marbury
Dodson, Walter	Soldier, Ga. Cont. Line
Dodson, William	Soldier, Ga. Cont. Line
Doer, John	Soldier, Ga. Cont. Line
Dollar, Anson	Soldier in Ga. State Legion from the reduction of Augusta to the evacuation of Savannah; served under command of Lt. Col. James Jackson
Dooly, Benjamin	Refugee
Donald, Absalom	Soldier in Bn. of Minute Men
Dooly, George	Refugee Captain
Dooly, Hull	Lt. on board Cont. Galley
Dooly, John	Colonel; was cruely murdered in his own house while on parole; was deceased prior to Feb. 1784; survived by two sons, Thomas Dooly and John Mitchell Dooly
Dooly, Thomas	Was killed while in the Cont. service; had

	a brother, George Dooly
Doss, Joel	Refugee
Doughty, Hull	Lt. on board one of the State Galleys
Douglas, Alexander	Soldier in Bn. of Minute Men
Dowdy, Richard	Soldier at siege of Augusta
Dowling, Thomas	Soldier in Cont. Reg. under command of Leonard Marbury
Downs, Ambrose	Refugee
Downs, George	Refugee
Downs, William	Refugee
Dowse, Gideon	Refugee
Driver, Henry	Soldier in Bn. of Minute Men
Duckworth, Jeremiah	Served in the Revolution
Duffey, John	Private in Bn. of Minute Men
Dugan, Thomas	Captain of a Co. of Militia under command of Col. Elijah Clark
Duhart, John	Refugee in North Carolina
Duke, William	Lt. in Bn. of Minute Men
Dukes, Henry	Captain in Bn. of Minute Men
Dukes, Henry	Refugee
Dukes, James	Soldier in Bn. of Minute Men
Dukes, John Taylor Sr.	Refugee and Soldier in Bn. of Minute Men
Dumaphlin, Elijah	Soldier in Bn. of Minute Men
Dumass, Elijah	Soldier in Bn. of Minute Men
Duncan, James	First Lt. in Bn. of Minute Men
Duncan, James	Was a Lt. in Wilkes Co. Militia before joining Refugees in North Carolina
Duncan, Joseph	Captain in Bn. of Minute Men
Duncan, Matthew	Lt. in Bn. of Minute Men; was in last siege of Augusta
Dunkin, William	Soldier in Bn. of Minute Men
Dunkin, William	Soldier in Bn. of Minute Men
Dunmore, James	Soldier in Bn. of Minute Men
Dunn, Josiah	Appointed Col. of Richmond Co. prior to the siege of Augusta
Dunn, Nehemiah	Refugee
Dunnison, Elijah	Sergeant, 1st. Bn. of Minute Men

Dunsmore, James	Soldier in Bn. of Minute Men
Dunwoody, James	Refugee Doctor
Dyer, Henry	Soldier in Bn. of Minute Men
Eanest, William	Refugee
Eaton, Peter	Soldier, Ga. Cont. Line
Eaves, Nathaniel	Enlisted on September 22, 1776, for three years by Lt. Wade of Captain Jeter's Co., 3rd. Bn., Ga. Cont. Troops (commanded by Lt. Col. John McIntosh); was discharged on August 26, 1779 as "he was very sickly and had engaged another man to serve the remainder of his time." Description of Eaves: age, 27; about 5 ft., 6 or 7 in. high; brown complexion; short black hair; born in Brunswick Co., Virginia
Eckles, Ephriam	Soldier in Rawleigh P. Downman's Co. of Infantry, 3rd. Reg., Cont. Troops of Ga.; Eckles died while in service
Edwards, James	Soldier in Reg. under command of Col. Leonard Marbury
Edwards, John	Soldier in Reg. under command of Col. Leonard Marbury
Edwards, John	Refugee in North Carolina
Eigle, John	Refugee
Eimbeck, George	"These certify that Mr. Eimbeck engaged in the service of the U.S. as a Sargent early in the year 1776 and in consequence of his faithful service was recommended by the officers of his Regiment to me for promotion in pursuance of which I appointed him in 1778 to be Barrack Master which duty he preformed with integrity and has ever since continued to act in to the close of the war and I am of opinion that the appointment of Barrack Master gives the rank of Captain but am not cer-

	tain. /S/ S. Elbert, Br. Gen., Cont. Army, Savannah, Ga., March 10, 1784."
Elliott, Daniel	Private, 2nd. Bn., Ga. Cont. Line; lost his life while serving therein; survived by wife, Elizabeth Elliott
Elliott, Henry	Refugee
Elliott, John	Refugee
Ellis, Robert	Soldier, 4th. Ga. Bn.
Ellis, William	Refugee
Ellison, James	Refugee
Ellrood, Conrod	Soldier in Bn. of Minute Men
Elridge, John	Soldier, Ga. Cont. Line
Elridge, Thomas	Soldier, Ga. Cont. Line
Elvin, John	Soldier in Reg. under command of Col. Leonard Marbury
Emanuel, Amos	Refugee
Emanuel, Asa	Refugee under Brig. Gen. John Twiggs in North Carolina
Emanuel, David	Refugee Captain
Emanuel, Levi	Militia Soldier and Refugee Sergeant Major in North Carolina
Espey, Thomas	Refugee Captain
Espey, William	Refugee
Eustace, John Skey	Major in the American Army
Evans, Archibald	Soldier in Reg. under command of Col. Leonard Marbury
Evans, Benjamin	Sergeant, 1st. Cont. Reg., Light Dragoons of Ga.; discharged on March 9, 1779
Evans, Daniel	Soldier, 2nd. Ga. Bn.
Evans, Daniel	Refugee
Evans, John	Sergeant, 1st. Co., (unnamed) Reg., Ga. Cont. Troops; enlisted in 1776 for the war and died in the service in 1780
Evans, Stephen	Refugee
Evans, William	Refugee
Evans, William	Soldier in Reg. under command of Col. Leonard Marbury

Fann, John	Refugee
Fann, William	Refugee
Farish, Robert	Lt., Reg. of Light Dragoons of Ga.; served from November 3, 1776 to January 8, 1780
Farling, Robert	Soldier, Ga. Cont. Line
Farmer, Asael	Refugee
Farrell, John	Soldier, Cont. Reg. of Light Horse of Ga., under command of Col. Leonard Marbury
Farrell, William	Lt. in Bn. of Minute Men under command of Col. Samuel Jack
Fenton, James	Soldier, Ga. Cont. Line
Ferrill, William	Soldier, Ga. Cont. Line
Ferrill, William	Refugee
Few, Benjamin	Refugee and Militia Colonel; was commander over the Ga. Militia and the South Carolina Militia
Few, William	Refugee Lt. Col.
Finly, William	Soldier, Ga. Cont. Line
Fleming, James	Refugee Major
Fleming, William	Soldier, Ga. Cont. Line
Flennikin, James	Private Soldier under command of Col. Elijah Clark
Fling, John	Soldier
Flowers, William	Soldier in one of the Ga. Bn. commanded by Col. Steward
Flowers, William	Soldier, 1st Bn. of Minute Men
Floyd, Pinmon	Soldier in Bn. of Minute Men
Flynn, James	Refugee
Folkson, Charles	"This is to certify that Charles Folkson is a man that left the British trups the 26th of July past, and joined the Mereken armys in the State of Georgia and that he has a wife and one child and a man that came with him to his family, and is now in real need of assistance to support himself and family. Richmond County., Feb-

	ruary 2, 1782."
Folson, Lawrence	Soldier in Bn. of Minute Men
Ford, John	Refugee
Ford, William	Refugee
Foster, Francis	Refugee; served under Col. Elijah Clark and fell in action at the siege of Augusta; survived by wife, Pennellepey Foster and no children
Foster, William	Refugee
France, Abram	Refugee
Francis, Charles	Soldier in Reg. of Dragoons
Francis, Frederick	Refugee
Frazer, Andrew	Refugee in Col. James McNiel's Bn.
Frazier, John	"This is to certify that Mr. John Frazer served as a Lt. in the line of this state from January, 1777 till 1st. July, 1782, when he was deranged. /S/ John Habersham, Major, late Cont. Line Savannah, 18th January, 1785."
Freeman, Holman	Refugee Adjutant
Freeman, James	Refugee
Freeman, John	Refugee
Freeman, William	Refugee
Friday, John	Soldier in Reg. under command of Col. Leonard Marbury
Frier, John	Soldier in Bn. of Minute Men
Frigonier, Conrad	Private, 1st. Bn., Ga. Cont. Line
Fuller, Isaac	Refugee from Richmond Co., Ga.
Fuller, Stephen	Refugee; joined Col. William Candler's Reg. at the first siege of Augusta; came in with Col. Clark to the last siege of Augusta before Grierson's Fort was taken
Fulsom, Benjamin	Captain in Bn. of Minute Men
Fulsome, Lawrence	Soldier in Bn. of Minute Men
Fulton, John	Refugee
Fulton, Samuel	Refugee Captain
Fulton, Samuel Jr.	Private in Bn. of Minute Men

Fulton, Samuel Sr.	Private, Col. Samuel Jack's Bn. of Minute Men
Fussell, Ezra	Refugee to North Carolina
Fussell, Thomas	Refugee
Gaines, Absalom	Soldier in Bn. of Minute Men
Gaines, Absalom	Soldier in Captain Henry Duke's Co., Col. John Stuart's Bn. of Minute Men
Gaines, Bailey	Soldier in Captain Henry Duke's Co., Col. John Stuart's Bn. of Minute Men
Gaines, Bailey	Soldier in Bn. of Minute Men
Gamble, John	Refugee in North Carolina after the fall of Charleston
Garnett, Eli	Refugee
Gaster, John	Soldier in Bn. of Minute Men
Gaston, Alexander	Lt. in Bn. of Minute Men commanded by Col. Samuel Jack; was deceased prior to March 1784
Gaston, David	Sergeant in Bn. of Minute Men
Gay, Aken	Refugee
Gay, Dennis	Soldier, Ga. Cont. Line
Gay, William	Soldier, Ga. Cont. Line
Gent, Charles	Refugee
Gent, William	Refugee
George, David	Soldier in Bn. of Minute Men
George, David	Soldier in Reg. of Dragoons
George, Denny	Soldier in Bn. of Minute Men
George, Isaac	Soldier in Bn. of Minute Men
George, John	Soldier in Bn. of Minute Men
George, Silas	Soldier in Bn. of Minute Men
George, Solomon	Soldier in Bn. of Minute Men
Gibbs, Richard	Soldier in Bn. of Minute Men
Gibbs, William	Soldier in the Ga. Line
Gibson, John	Served in the Revolution
Gideons, Francis	Refugee Captain under command of Col. Elijah Clarke
Gideons, William	Militia Soldier and Refugee under command of Col. Elijah Clarke

Gift, Jonathan	Refugee in North Carolina
Giles, Arthur	Private in Bn. of Minute Men under command of Col. Samuel Jack
Giles, Samuel	Refugee
Giles, William	Private in Bn. of Minute Men under command of Col. Samuel Jack
Gilliland, Hugh	Refugee under command of Col. Elijah Clarke
Gilliland, William	Refugee
Gillion, Joshua	Soldier in Bn. of Minute Men
Gillison, Peter	Soldier in Bn. of Minute Men
Girardeau, John	Refugee
Girardeau, William	Refugee
Glascock, Thomas	Lt. in the Ga. Cont. Line
Glass, Joel	Militia Soldier under command of Captain Gunnells
Glass, Joshua	Militia Soldier under command of Captain Gunnells
Gloveyer, Hardy	Does not say he was in service; but, "was taken a prisoner by British Troops immediately after the first siege of Augusta—carried to Charleston and died a prisoner."
Gloveyer, Stephen	Refugee Lt.
Godbe, Cary	Refugee
Godbe, William	Refugee
Goldwire, James	Refugee
Goodall, Plesant	Refugee
Gordon, Jesse	Soldier in Bn. of Minute Men
Gore, Thomas	Soldier in Bn. of Minute Men
Gorham, John	Private in Bn. of Minute Men
Goulding, Peter	Refugee
Gragg, Thomas	Refugee
Graham, William	Private in Col. George Walton's Reg., Militia; then he was a Refugee; later he was in the North Carolina Militia; he was "at Eutaa's had the command of a platoon in the center, where he lost six men out of fif-

	teen, and was one of the party that took the first field piece from the enemy and every man belonging to it put to instant death;" he was in the field from the repulse at Camden until the evacuation of Savannah; he saw much service, especially at Gillford and the Eutaas
Grant, John	Captain in Col. Asa Emanuel's Reg., Militia; enlisted on August 19, 1781 and served until "he unfortunately fell in battle at the White house on Ogeache, he being at the time detached with this Company under the command of Col. James Jackson. . . ."
Grant, Peter	Refugee in North Carolina after the reduction of Charleston by the British Troops
Gravat, Obediah	Private, 3rd. Ga. Bn.
Graves, John	Refugee; lived in Sunbury, Ga.
Gray, James	Soldier in Bn. of Minute Men
Gray, John	Soldier in Bn. of Minute Men
Gray, Richard	Cont. Soldier
Greasell, George	Served under Lt. Col. James Jackson in Ga. State Legion
Green, Andrew M.	Soldier in Bn. of Minute Men
Green, Benjamin	Refugee
Green, Henry	Soldier
Green, John	Refugee Lt.
Green, Joshua	Soldier in Bn. of Minute Men
Green, McKeen	Refugee
Green, Thomas	Private in Bn. of Minute Men
Green, William	Refugee in North Carolina after the reduction of Charleston by Brtish Troops
Greer, Robert	Lt. in Bn. of Minute Men
Gregg, Thomas	Refugee
Grey, Robert M.	Soldier in Bn. of Minute Men
Grier, Robert	Lt. in Bn. of Minute Men
Grier, Robert	Refugee

Grier, Thomas	Refugee
Griffin, Randal	Refugee
Griffin, Samuel	Soldier in Bn. of Minute Men
Grimsley, Elijah	Sergeant in Bn. of Minute Men
Griner, Philip	Refugee
Grizzel, John	Soldier in Bn. of Minute Men
Grubbs, Danny	Soldier in Bn. of Minute Men
Gruen, Andrew M.	Soldier in Bn. of Minute Men
Gunnels, Nicholas	Soldier in Bn. of Minute Men
Guy, John	Soldier, Ga. Cont. Line
Hadden, William	Refugee in North Carolina
Hadding, James	Soldier, Ga. Cont. Line
Hadding, William	Soldier, Ga. Cont. Line
Hager, James	Soldier in Bn. of Minute Men
Haile, Edward	Private in Bn. of Minute Men; "This is to certify that Susanna Haile is the widdow of Edard Haile who died in the Flouraday expedition, in the service of this State and have three children under the age of fourteen. . . ."
Hall, Benjamin	Refugee
Hall, James	Private in Bn. of Minute Men
Hammack, Robert	Refugee
Hambleton, James	Soldier in Bn. of Minute Men
Hamilton, Thomas	Refugee; "was taken in Charles Town"
Hammond, Charles	Refugee under command of Col. William Candler; was in the first siege of Augusta
Hammond, George	Refugee under command of Col. William Candler; was in the first siege of Augusta
Hampton, John	Refugee
Hancock, William	Soldier in Reg. under command of Col. Leonard Marbury
Handshaw, Thomas	"This is to certify that Thomas Handshaw was a soldier in my company in the first Regiment of Georgia, in Continental service and served his time in the said regiment till he lost his eye sight. September

	24, 1785. /S/ G. Handley, Capt. in the late Geo. Reg."
Hannah, Thomas	Refugee under command of Col. Elijah Clarke
Hardy, Ephriam	Soldier, Ga. Cont. Line
Hardy, James	Soldier, Ga. Cont. Line
Hardy, John	Soldier, Ga. Cont. Line
Hardy, John	Served three years in Ga. as Captain of a Cont. Galley
Hardy, Robert	Soldier, Ga. Cont. Line
Harley, James	Soldier, Ga. Cont. Line
Harper, Joseph	Sergeant in Bn. of Minute Men
Harper, Robert	Refugee Lt.
Harper, Samuel	Refugee Captain
Harris, Buckner	Refugee
Harris, David	Refugee
Harris, David	Refugee Captain
Harris, John	Soldier in Reg. under command of Col. Leonard Marbury
Harris, John	Refugee
Harris, Samuel	Refugee
Harris, Tyree Glen	Soldier, 3rd. Bn.; enlisted by Captain Thomas Scott; discharged by Captain Thomas Threadgill
Harrison, Walter	Soldier, Ga. Cont. Line
Harrod, Robert	Soldier, Ga. Cont. Line
Hart, John	Refugee
Hartford, James	Soldier, Ga. Cont. Line
Hartford, John	Soldier, Ga. Cont. Line
Harvey, James	Refugee
Harvey, Joel	Refugee
Harvey, John	Soldier in Bn. of Minute Men
Harvey, John	Refugee
Harvey, Littleberry	Refugee under command of Co. M. Williamson; returned to this state and served in the siege of Augusta
Harvill, Joseph	Refugee under command of Col. William

Hatcher, Archibald	Captian in one of the state Galleys
Hatcher, Henry	Refugee under command of Col. William Candler
Hatcher, Jeremiah	Refugee under command of Col. William Candler
Hatcher, John	Refugee under command of Col. William Candler
Hatcher, Josiah	Refugee in the northern states
Hatcher, Robert	Refugee under command of Col. William Candler
Hatcher, William	Refugee under command of Col. William Candler
Hatchet, Archibald	Captain in one of the State Galleys; died while in the service
Hatwell, Luther	Refugee
Hawkins, Cesar	Soldier, 1st. Bn. of Minute Men
Hawkins, James	Soldier, Ga. State Legion, under command of Lt. Col. James Jackson
Hawkins, Nicholas	Soldier, Ga. State Legion, under command of Lt. Col. James Jackson
Hawkins, Noel	Soldier in Bn. of Minute Men
Hawkins, Thomas	Refugee
Hawthorn, Stephen	Refugee
Haylewood, Richard	Soldier in Bn. of Minute Men
Hayman, Henry	Refugee
Hayman, Stephen	Refugee
Hayman Stouton	Refugee
Hays, James	Soldier in Col. Samuel Jack's Bn.; was discharged on July 27, 1778
Heally, Henry	Soldier, Ga. State Legion, under command of Lt. Col. James Jackson
Heard, Benard	Refugee
Heard, Joseph	Refugee
Heard, Richard	Refugee Captain
Heard, Stephen	Refugee
Hearn, John	Soldier, Ga. Cont. Line

Heart, Richard	Soldier, Ga. Cont. Line
Heath, Francis	Soldier in Bn. of Minute Men
Heatley, Robert	Private in Bn. of Minute Men
Heckerson, John	Soldier in Reg. of Dragoons
Hemby, Dennis	Refugee
Henderson, Zachariah	Soldier in Bn. of Minute Men and Militia Soldier
Henley, John	Soldier, Ga. Cont. Line
Henson, Samuel	Refugee
Herd, George	Refugee
Hertford, William	Soldier, Ga. Cont. Line
Hews, Nicholas	Soldier in Bn. of Minute Men
Hicks, Isaac	Captain, 3rd. Ga. Cont. Reg.; was commissioned in 1776 and served thereafter until the end of the war
Hicks, John	Refugee
Higgins, Nicholas	Soldier in Bn. of Minute Men
Hill, James	Refugee
Hill, James	Soldier in Bn. of Minute Men
Hill, Joshua	Refugee
Hill, Peter	Soldier in Bn. of Minute Men
Hill, William	Refugee
Hillary, Christopher	Lt., Cont. Army
Hodge, John	Refugee
Hodge, Robert	Refugee
Hodge, Roger	Refugee
Hodge, Willoughby	Refugee
Hogg, James	Soldier; was at the siege of Augusta
Hogg, Samuel	Soldier in Bn. of Minute Men
Hoggatt, John	Sergeant, 3rd. Ga. Bn.
Hogges, James	Soldier in Bn. of Minute Men
Holland, Thomas	Soldier in Bn. of Minute Men
Holliday, Ambrose	Refugee under command of Col. William Candler
Holliday, Thomas	Refugee
Holliday, William	Refugee
Holloman, Absalom	Refugee

Holt, Beverly	Private, 2nd. Reg., Ga. Line; served three years
Holt, Reuben	Soldier, 2nd. Reg., Ga. Cont. Line; died while on duty in the 2nd. Ga.
Holton, Francis	Private, 1st. Bn. of Minute Men
Holtzendorf, William	Refugee
Horn, Absolom	"I certify that I am informed Absolom Horn was killed in the besieging (of) Augusta as was esteemed a person true to the American cause and has left a distressed widow and four small children. January 24, 1782. /S/ Isaac Skinner, Capt."
Horner, John	Soldier, Ga. Cont. Line
Hornsby, Phillip	Refugee
House, John	Private, 3rd. Cont. Reg., Ga. Line; enlisted by Lt. Thomas Threadgill in said Reg. on September 6, 1776 for three years; received $10.00 bounty at time of enlistment; discharged September 7, 1779
Housley, Welden	Sergeant in Bn. of Minute Men
Houston, Henry	Soldier in Bn. of Minute Men
Houston, William	Soldier in Bn. of Minute Men
Houstoun, James	"This certifys that James Houston, Esquire, was appointed Surgeon to the 1st. Georgia Continental Regiment of infantry the 3rd. April, 1776 and continued in the service during the war. February 26, 1784. Lachn. McIntosh, M. General."
Howard, Charles	Soldier in Bn. of Minute Men
Howard, John	Soldier in Bn. of Minute Men
Howell, Caleb	Refugee
Howell, Daniel	Refugee Captain
Hubbard, Jacob	Refugee
Hubbard, John	Refugee
Hudson, James	Refugee in 1779, 1780, and 1781
Hudson, Joseph	Refugee
Hudson, Nathaniel	Refugee

Hudson, Robert	Refugee
Hudson, Samuel	Refugee
Huggens, Robert	Soldier in Bn. of Minute Men
Hughes, Isaac	Private in Bn. of Minute Men
Hughes, Nathaniel	Lt., Captain Lee's Co., Ga. Artillery deceased prior to September 1784 and survived by heir, Elizabeth Watson
Hughs, John	Private in Bn. of Minute Men
Hunt, Fitz Maurice	Refugee
Hunt, Thomas	Soldier in Reg. under command of Col. Leonard Marbury
Hunt, William	Refugee
Hunt, William	Soldier in Bn. of Minute Men
Huntsman, William	Refugee
Hutts, John	Soldier in Bn. of Minute Men
Idole, Henery	Soldier in Reg. under command of Col. Leonard Marbury
Igle, John	Refugee
Ingles, John	Soldier in Reg. under command of Col. Leonard Marbury
Inlow, Potter	Private in Bn. of Minute Men
Inman, Joshua	Refugee Captain in North Carolina
Inman, Shadrack	Refugee Captain; killed in action
Jack, Samuel	Refugee
Jackson, Daniel	Refugee
Jackson, Isaac	Refugee Major
Jackson, Isaac	Soldier, Cont. Reg. under command of Col. Leonard Marbury
Jackson, James	Refugee Major and Lt. Col.
Jackson, John	Soldier, 1st. Bn. of Minute Men
Jackson, Michael	Soldier, Cont. Reg. of Light Horse, under command of Col. Leonard Marbury
Jackson, Reuben	Soldier in Bn. of Minute Men
Jackson, Robert	Soldier in Reg. under command of Col. Leonard Marbury
Jackson, Simon	Soldier, 3rd. Ga. Bn.
Jackson, William	Soldier, Ga. Cont. Line

James, Absolom	Soldier in Bn. of Minute Men
James, John	Soldier in Lt. Col. Leonard Marbury's Reg.
James, John	Soldier in Reg. of Dragoons
Jarvis, Nicholas	Refugee
Jefferson, Isaac	Refugee
Jeffries, James	Refugee
Jenkins, Benjamin	Refugee
Jenkins, Elijah	Refugee
Jenkins, Francis	Refugee
Jenkins, George	Soldier in Bn. of Minute Men
Jenkins, Robert	Cont. Soldier
Jenkins, Sherwood	Soldier in Bn. of Minute Men
Jenkins, Thomas	Refugee
Jenkins, William	Soldier, Cont. Reg. of Light Dragoons under command of Col. Leonard Marbury
Jenkinson, Robert	Soldier in Reg. under command of Col. Leonard Marbury
Johns, James	Soldier, Cont. Reg. of Light Dragoons under command of Col. Leonard Marbury
Johns, Peter	Refugee
Johns, Ware	Soldier in Reg. under command of Col. Leonard Marbury
Johnson, Daniel	Sergeant in Bn. of Minute Men
Johnson, James	Sergeant, Capt. Sham Thompson's Co., Col. Samuel Jack's Bn. of Minute Men
Johnson, John	Refugee Captain
Johnson, Richard	Refugee Captain in F. Hammon's Reg.
Johnson, Stephen	Refugee Captain
Johnson, Stephen	Soldier, 3rd. Ga. Bn.
Johnson, Thomas	Refugee Lt.
Johnson, William	Soldier, 1st. Bn. of Minute Men
Johnson, William	Soldier in Bn. of Minute Men
Johnson, William	Refugee
Johnston, David	Soldier, 1st. Bn. of Minute Men
Johnston, Isaac	Soldier in Bn. of Minute Men
Johnston, James	Sergeant in Bn. of Minute Men

Johnston, John H.	Refugee
Johnston, John Hutchins	Soldier
Johnston, Levy	Soldier in Bn. of Minute Men
Johnston, Richard	Soldier and Militia Soldier at the siege and capture of Augusta in June 1781
Johnston, Silas	Soldier in Bn. of Minute Men
Johnston, William	"This is to certify that Mr. William Johnston was appointed as Ensign in the first Continental Battalion of this state in 1776, afterwards a second Lieutenant in the same, and lastly Captain Lieut. of the 1st. Company of Artillery, and that he died in 1780 a prioser of War, as I am credibly informed. Savannah, 11th. March, 1784. /S/ John Habersham, Major of the late Geo. Line."
Johnston, William	Refugee
Joiner, Benjamin	Refugee
Jolly, Thomas	Soldier, Ga. Cont. Line
Jones, Able	Soldier in Reg. under command of Col. Leonard Marbury
Jones, Abraham	Refugee
Jones, Aventon	Soldier in Bn. of Minute Men
Jones, David	Militia Soldier
Jones, David	Soldier in Bn. of Minute Men
Jones, Dyal	Soldier in Bn. of Minute Men
Jones, Edward	Refugee
Jones, Jacob	Soldier in Reg. under command of Col. Leonard Marbury
Jones, James	Private in Col. Samuel Jack's Bn. of Minute Men; went on Florida expedition
Jones, James	Refugee
Jones, Jesse	Refugee
Jones, Jesse	Soldier in Bn. of Minute Men
Jones, John	Refugee Lt. Col.
Jones, John	Soldier in Bn. of Minute Men
Jones, John	Soldier in Reg. under command of Col.

	Leonard Marbury
Jones, Matthew	Refugee
Jones, Michael	Refugee Captain in North Carolina
Jones, Noel	Soldier in Bn. of Minute Men
Jones, Peter	Soldier in Bn. of Minute Men
Jones, Richard	Enlisted in Bn. of Minute Men by Major Caleb Howell in South Carolina; served as a soldier therein until after the Florida expedition
Jones, Robert	Soldier, Ga. State Legion Infantry, under command of Lt. Col. James Jackson
Jones, Russell	Soldier, Reg. of Cont. Light Dragoons under command of Lt. Col. Leonard Marbury
Jones, Seaborn	Refugee
Jones, Solomon	Soldier in Bn. of Minute Men
Jones, Thomas	Refugee; was the son of William Jones
Jones, Thomas	Soldier in Reg. under command of Col. Leonard Marbury
Jones, Turner	Soldier in Reg. under command of Col. Leonard Marbury
Jones, William	Soldier, Ga. State Legion, under command of Lt. Col. James Jackson
Jordan, Jacob	Refugee
Josling, Daniel	Refugee; served in Reg. under command of Col. William Candler
Kasey, Stephen Jr.	Refugee
Keelock, Ebenezer	Soldier in Bn. of Minute Men
Kellock, John	Soldier in Bn. of Minute Men
Kelly, Jacob	Refugee
Kelly, John	Refugee
Kelsey, Hugh	Sergeant, Col. Samuel Jack's Bn. of Minute Men
Kelsey, Thomas	Private, Col. Samuel Jack's Bn. of Minute Men; was deceased prior to February 1784
Kemp, William	Refugee

Kendrick, Hezikiah	Refugee under command of Col. William Candler
Kersey, Stephen	Refugee
Kilpatrick, Thomas	Refugee
Kimbrough, Shadrick	Militia Soldier
Kimbry, John	Lt. Captain Heard's Co.
King, Henry	Soldier in Bn. of Minute Men
King, John	Private, 1st. Reg., Ga. Cont. Troops, commanded by Major Handley; enlisted for duration and served until the end of war
King, Peter	Soldier in Reg. under command of Col. Leonard Marbury
Kinnebrew, Jacob	Soldier
Kirk, Thomas	Was in military service in Ga.
Kirkham, Joseph	Soldier, Ga. State Legion, under command of Lt. Col. James Jackson
Kitchens, John	Soldier, Captain Michael Dicksen's Co., Col. Samuel Jack's Bn. of Minute Men
Kitts, John	Soldier, Col. Samuel Jack's Reg. of Minute Men
Kook, Robert	Soldier in Reg. under command of Col. Leonard Marbury
Lackey, William	Refugee
Lam, Thomas	Refugee
Lamar, Luke	Soldier in Bn. of Minute Men
Lamar, Zachariah	Refugee
Lambeth, William	Lt. on board one of the Ga. Galleys; died while in service; survived by heir, Elizabeth Watson
Lambreech, John	Refugee
Lancaster, Rowling	Soldier, 2nd. Bn., Cont. Troops; died while in service
Landers, Jacob	Refugee
Lane, James	Soldier, 3rd. Ga. Bn.; enlisted for three years, which time he served, except for three months furlough he had given him by his commanding officer for the recov-

	ery of his health
Lane, Joseph	Was an officer in the Ga. Line
Lane, Thomas	Refugee in 1779, 1780, 1781 and 1782
Lane, William	Soldier, 3rd. Ga. Bn., Cont. Troops; enlisted for three years and died in service before his enlishment was up
Langton, David	Soldier in Bn. of Minute Men
Lanier, Benjamin	Refugee
Lanier, Clement	Refugee
Lanier, Lemuel	Refugee
Lanier, Samuel	Refugee in Virginia
Lankford, Moses	"Virginia, Decr. 29th., 1782. This is to certify that Moses Lankford enlisted as a soldier in my company for three years and that he hath served his time out—therefore is discharged from the said service. Given under my hand the date above mentioned. /S/ Isaac Hicks, Capt., 3rd. Georgia C. Battalion."
Lankford, Parish	"This is to certify that Parish Lankford of Mecklinburg County enlisted as a soldier in my company the 21th. day of January, 1777 to serve three years in the Continental service, and that he has served his time out as a good soldier. Given under my hand this 12th. day of August, 1780. /S/ Isaac Hicks, Capt., 3rd. Georgia Contn. Battan."
Lauderdale, John	Refugee
Law, George	Refugee
Lawrence, Peter	Soldier in Bn. of Minute Men
Lawson, Andrew	Refugee in North Carolina
Lawson, Andrew	Private in Col. Asa Emanuel's Reg., Burke County Militia; "These are to certify that Andrew Lawson did steadfastly do his duty as a good soldier and faithfull citizen of this state from the 19th. of August, 1781

	until he fell in November following at Gov. Wright's White House onver Ogeche, then under command of Lt. Col. James Jackson. Given this 15th day of March, 1784. /S/ John Twiggs, Brig. Gen."
Lawson, Hugh	Refugee Captain
Lawson, John Jr.	Refugee; was a prisoner most of the time
Lawson, Roger Jr.	Refugee in North Carolina
Lawson, Thomas	Soldier in Bn. of Minute Men
Lazarus, Nicholas	Soldier, Ga. Line
Ledbetter, John	Refugee
Lee, Andrew	Refugee
Lee, Timothy	Refugee
Legett, Abner	Refugee
Legett, John	Refugee under command of Col. Elijah Clarke
Legett, John	Soldier, 1st. Bn. of Minute Men
Lemar, Gedeon	Soldier in Reg. of Dragoons under command of Col. Leonard Marbury
Lett, James	"I do certify that James Lett deceas's served as a private in my Regt. of Militia in the State of Georgia from the 19th. Day of August, 1781 until he fell in battle at Govr. Wight's Plantation on Ogeache, he being under the command of Colo. James Jackson... He has left a widow and some small children in Burke County. Given under my hand at Savannah 15th. day of January, 1784. /S/ Asa Emanuel, then Col., Burke County Militia;" James Lett survived by wife, Hannah Lett, and children
Lett, Patrick	Soldier in Reg. of Dragoons
Lett, Reubin	Refugee in North Carolina
Lett, Reubin	Soldier in Bn. of Minute Men
Levellon, James	Soldier, 1st. Bn. of Minute Men
Levellon, William	Soldier, 1st. Bn. of Minute Men

Leverett, Henry	Refugee
Leverett, John	Soldier under command of Col. Elijah Clarke; was killed by the enemy while in the service
Leverett, Robert	Refugee
Leverite, Aaron	Soldier
Levins, Richard	Refugee
Levins, Richard	Soldier, 1st. Bn. of Minute Men
Lewis, Benjamin	Refugee in North Carolina
Lewis, David	Refugee; was deceased prior to April 1784; survived by widow, Kesiah Lewis
Lewis, David Jr.	Refugee
Lewis, Eliezer	Refugee
Lewis, Evan Dr.	Surgeons Mate in the hospitals of the Southern Cont. Army and "he served to the time of his death;" was a citizen of Ga. and a doctor; survived by two brothers, Thomas and Jacob Lewis (also see Joel Lewis below)
Lewis, Jacob	Refugee in North Carolina
Lewis, Joel	Refugee; returned to Ga. about the time of retaking of Augusta and was unfortunately killed by a party of Tories; survived by two brothers, Thomas and Jacob Lewis; was also brother to Dr. Evan Lewis, deceased (see above)
Lewis, Josiah, Rev.	Refugee Chaplain; died on November 10, 1784; survived by wife, Susanna and the following children: Jonathan Kees Lewis, aged about 10; Benjamin Thomas Lewis, aged about 8; Susanna Lewis, aged about 3; Josiah Lewis, aged about 1 (ages in August 1784)
Lewis, Thomas	Refugee in North Carolina
Liles, George	Soldier in Reg. under command of Col. Leonard Marbury
Linden, Joseph	Sergeant in Ga. Cont Line; died on board

	a prison ship; survived by wife, Marey Linden
Lindsay, Dennis	Refugee
Lindsay, John	Refugee Major
Linn, Robert	Soldier in Reg. under command of Col. Leonard Marbury
Linton, John	Militia Soldier
Lipham, Frederick	Lt. in Bn. of Minute Men
Lithgow, Andrew Jr.	Private in Bn. of Minute Men
Lithgow, Andrew Sr.	Private, 2nd. Bn. of Minute Men
Lithgow, Robert	Soldier in Bn. of Minute Men
Little, David	Militia Soldier
Little, James	Refugee
Lockhart, Isaac	Refugee
Logan, Phillip	Refugee under command of Col. Elijah Clark
Long, John	Soldier in Bn. of Minute Men
Lowe, Daniel	Private in Bn. of Minute Men
Lowe, Obadiah	Refugee
Lowe, Philip	Major, Ga. Line
Lucas, John	Major, Ga. Line
Lucas, William	Refugee
Luck, Asa	Soldier; deceased prior to May 1784
Luck, John	Soldier; deceased prior to May 1784
Lunday, Theophilus	Refugee
Lyle, William	Soldier, Ga. Cont. Line
Lynch, John	Soldier, 2nd. Ga. Bn.; enlisted on September 1, 1776 to serve three years under command of Captain and Paymaster Littleberry Mosby
Lynn, Curtis	Soldier in Captain Isaac Hick's Co., 3rd. Ga. Reg.; Lynn resided in Sussex Co., Virginia in January 1785
Lynn, John	Soldier, 3rd. Ga. Cont. Bn.; deceased prior to January 1785
Lynn, John	Soldier in Captain George Handley's Co., 1st. Ga. Reg.

Maban, Matthew	Soldier in Col. Samuel Jack's Bn. of Minute Men; was residing in Rutherford Co., North Carolina in February 1786
Mabry, Reps	"Virginia, 18th. Feby, 1783—This is to certify that Reps Mabry of North Carolina enlisted as Sargent in my company to serve three years in the Continental Army, and that he hath served his full time out, given under my hand the day and date above mentioned. /S/ Isaac Hicks, Capt., in the 3rd. Contn. Battalion."
Maddox, John	Refugee
Maden, David	Refugee
Madin, Dennis	Soldier in Bn. of Minute Men
Mahon, Archibald	Soldier in Bn. of Minute Men
Maise, John	Soldier
Maise, Joseph	Sergent, 2nd. Ga. Cont. Reg.
Mallard, Lazarus	Refugee
Manadue, Henry	Refugee Captain
Mann, John	Refugee in South Carolina
Mann, Martin	"I certify that Martin Mann served as a spy on the frontiers of Georgia from the 18th. Octr., 1778 to the 30th November following at twenty pounds Georgia money. /S/ A.C. Vinson (?)."
Manning, John	Soldier, Cont. Light Horse of Ga.
Manning, Robert	Refugee
Mannon, William	Soldier, 1st. Bn. of Minute Men
Marbury, Horatio	Refugee under command of Col. Elijah Clarke
Marbury, Leonard	Refugee Col.
Marbury, Thomas	Refugee
Marcas, Thomas	Soldier in Bn. of Minute Men
Marshall, Abraham, Rev.	Chaplain in Col. Stewart's Reg. of Minute Men and in Gen. Williamson's Brigade when lying in camp opposite Augusta; Marshall was also a Refugee Chaplain

Martin, Cornelious	Soldier in Bn. of Minute Men
Martin, Edmond	Refugee Lt. under command of Col. William Candler; joined Col. Chandler's Reg. at 1st. siege of Augusta
Martin, James	Refugee Second Lt. in Reg. under command of Col. William Candler
Martin, James	Refugee Lt. Col. in Reg. under command of Col. William Candler
Martin, John	Refugee Lt. Col. and Lt. Col. in the Chatham Co. Reg., commanded by Col. George Walton
Martin, John Jr.	Refugee in North Carolina
Martin, Marshall	Refugee Private under command of Col. William Candler; joined Col. Candler's Reg. at 1st. siege of Augusta
Martin, Matt	Refugee Private under command of Col. William Candler
Martin, Simon	Refugee under command of Col. William Candler
Martin, William	First Lt., 1st. Bn. of Minute Men
Mash, Thomas	Soldier in Bn. of Minute Men
Mash, Thomas	Private, Captain Henry Duke's Co., Col. John Stuart's Bn. of Minute Men
Mathews, Daniel	Private in Bn. of Minute Men
Mathews, Daniel Jr.	Private in Bn. of Minute Men
Matthews, Isham	Private in Bn. of Minute Men
Matthews, Isum	Refugee
Matthews, Reubin	Private in Bn. of Minute Men
Matthews, William	Was in Co. of Musters; "Haddrell's Point, the 5th. Novemr., 1780. This certifys that Mr. William Matthews was appointed by an order of Major General Howe, early in the month of January, 1778, assistant to Lieut. Col. William Massey, Deputy Muster-Master General for the States of South Carolina and Georgia with the rank of Captain, to be obeyed and respected ac-

cordingly. NB: Capt. Mathews was made prisoner on the 29. December, 1778. /S/ John Habersham, Major, 1st. C. B. Georgia."

Matthews, William	Private in Bn. of Minute Men
Matthews, William	Refugee
Mattox, Benjamin	Private in Bn. of Minute Men commanded by Col. Samuel Jack
Mattox, John	Private in Captain Shame Thomson's Co., Bn. of Minute Men commanded by Col. Samuel Jack
Mattox, William	Private in Bn. of Minute Men commanded by Col. Samuel Jack
Maxwell, Bazil	Soldier, 2nd. Bn. Cont. Troops of Ga.; enlisted for three years and died while in service
Maxwell, Josiah	"Josiah Maxwell has produced several officers as evidence that he was an officer in the Continental Service the beginning of the year, 1778 and he asserts upon honor himself that he was appointed as Ensign in the Third Georgia Continental Regiment the 5th. January, 1778 and was promoted to a Lieutenancy in the same regiment the 2nd. May, following, in which capacity he served to my own knowledge until he retired in January, 1783, but says he lost his Brevets with all his baggage when Savannah was taken. Given under my hand at Savannah this 14th. January, 1781. /S/ Lachn. McIntosh, Major General."
Maxwell, Thomas	Captain of one of the galleys of the Ga. Line
Maxwell, Thomas	Major, 1st. Bn. of Minute Men
Maxwell, Thomas	Refugee
May, Baily	Soldier in Bn. of Minute Men
May, William	Soldier in Bn. of Minute Men

Maben, Mathew	Private in Bn. of Minute Men
Maben, William	Private in Bn. of Minute Men
McBride, Edward	"This is to certify that Edward McBride was enlisted in the second Battn. of Georgia and was taken prisoner when Sunbury fell and lay aboard a British prisoner ship till the twenty eight of June and since that time as far as I can larn he has acted as an honest man. . . . /S/ John Morrison."
McCain, John	Refugee
McCall, Thomas	Refugee
McCalpin, Alexander	Refugee
McCalvey, John	Soldier in Bn. of Minute Men
McCalvey, William	Soldier in Bn. of Minute Men
McCardell, Cornelius	Soldier, 1st. Bn. of Minute Men
McCartee, William	Soldier, Ga. Cont. Line
McCarthy, John	Adjutant in the service from 1781 till end of war
McCarty, Daniel	Refugee
McCarty, John	Refugee
McCarty, John	Drum Major in Bn. of Minute Men; went on Florida expedition; was discharged at Midway Meeting House
McClendon, Joseph	Soldier in Bn. of Minute Men
McClendon, Traves	Refugee
McClum, Sampson	Soldier in Bn. of Minute Men
McCormack, Benjamin	Refugee
McCormack, Joseph	Refugee
McCoy, James	Refugee Captain
McCulloch, John	Refugee in North Carolina
McCulluck, David	Soldier in Bn. of Minute Men
McCulluck, Rodger	Soldier in Bn. of Minute Men
McCullough, Patrick	Private in Bn. of Minute Men
McCullough, Samuel	Sergeant in Captain Michael Dickson's Co., Col. Samuel Jack's Bn. of Minute Men; was residing in Camden District, South Carolina in February 1784

McDaniel, Takiah	Soldier in Bn. of Minute Men
McDonald, Hugh	Soldier in Bn. of Minute Men
McDowell, James	Served three years as a Private in the 2nd. Ga. Line
McDowell, Thomas	Lt.
McDowell, Thomas	Soldier in Bn. of Minute Men
McDowell, Thomas	Refugee
McGary, Edward	Refugee
McGary, Robert	Soldier, 1st. Bn. of Minute Men
McGee, Hugh	Refugee Captain
McGee, Lewis	Refugee
McGehee, Thomas	Soldier, Ga. State Legion under command of Lt. Col. James Jackson
McGill, John	Soldier in Bn. of Minute Men
McGilton, James	"I do certify Mr. James McGilton a refugee of Georgia, did make his escape from that state with me, when Charleston ware closely besieged, and expected to fall every day, and continued in his country's service, during the ware, only when a prisoner, and that was at the time Augusta ware besieged. Certified 8th. Day of March, 1784. /S/ William Farr, Lt. Col., Spartan Regiment."
McGilton, James	Soldier, Ga. Line
McGilton, Vance	Soldier, Ga. Line; was deceased prior to April 1784
McHainey, Terry	"This is to certify that Terry McHainey enlisted under me in the Third Georgia Battalion for three years, which time he served as a soldier. Witness my hand this 7th. March, 1785. /S/ Gedeon Booker, Captain, 3rd. Ga. Batt." McHainey was a Private
McHam, Nicolous	Soldier in Bn. of Minute Men
McIntosh, Lachlan	Major; was deceased prior to February 1785

McIntosh, Lachlan	Brigadier General, later Major General, Ga. Cont. Line
McIntosh, Peter	Soldier in Col. Benton's Reg. of Militia in South Carolina
McIntosh, William	Appointed Major by the Ga. Legislature to command a Reg. of Horse; appointment later confirmed by the Continental Congress
McKay, James	Captain
McKelvey, William	Soldier in Bn. of Minute Men
McKenney, Henry	Refugee
McKenney, Matthew	Private in Bn. of Minute Men
McKenney, Nathan	Soldier in Bn. of Minute Men
McKenney, Thomas	Soldier in Bn. of Minute Men
McKenney, William	Refugee
McKenney, William	Soldier in Bn. of Minute Men
McLain, James	Refugee
McLain, Joseph	Soldier, 2nd. Bn., Ga. Line
McLean, Lewis	"This is to certify that Lewis McLean served as a private soldier in Genl. Sumters Brigade of Militia from the 1st of June, 1780 till he was defeated on Fishing Creek in South Carolina. /S/ Francis Tennill, Major, Brigade."
McLendon, Joseph	Soldier in Bn. of Minute Men
McMan, Mathew	Soldier in Bn. of Minute Men
McMullen, Patrick	Private, 1st. Bn. of Minute Men
McMurphy, Daniel	Refugee in North Carolina
McMurray, Frederic	Soldier
McMurray, John	Soldier in Bn. of Minute Men
McMurray, Samuel	Served twelve months duty in the Revolutionary War under Captain Dixon against the Cherokee Indians at Phillips Fort in Georgia; survived by son, Alexander Blair
McMurray, William	Soldier in Bn. of Minute Men
McNair, Daniel	Served in the Revolution
McNatt, Solomon	Soldier, 1st. Bn. of Minute Men

McNeely, Daniel	Soldier under command of Gen. Twiggs
McNeely, Daniel	Refugee
McNeely, Daniel	Private in Bn. of MInute Men
McNeil, Archibald	"This is to certify that Archibald McNiel, Esquire deceased fell in the service of this Country as a Refugee from the State of Georgia. 2nd. of Feby, 1780. /S/ John Twiggs, B.G."
McNeil, James	Refugee Major
McNeil, Michael	Served in the Revolution
Melvin, George	Captain of the Ga. Line
Mercer, John	General of the Revolutionary Army
Mercer, Silas, Rev.	Refugee Chaplain with rank of Major; "This is to certify that the Revd. Silas Mercer in the beginning of these times was very active and useful in convincing the people of the justice of the cause of America and after the british took possession of Savannah he spent much of his time in preaching to the armies and obtained an excellent recommendation from Col. Hammond's to General Lincoln in order that he might preach to his army and as he was on his way to Purasburg he came to Burke jail to preach to my regiment and was there in the time of a very warm engagement and behaved himself exceeding well in time of action and soon afterwards he left the state at the expence of chief of his property rather than surrender to British Government.... /S/ Benjamin Few, Col. of Richmond Co."
Metcalf, Anthony	Lt. in Col. Samuel Jack's Bn. of Minute Men
Metcalf, Danza	Soldier in Col. Samuel Jack's Bn. of Minute Men
Metcalf, William	Soldier in Col. Samuel Jack's Bn. of Min-

	ute Men
Meyers, Thomas	Refugee
Michael, Frederick	Soldier in Reg. under command of Col. Leonard Marbury
Michael, John	Refugee and Wagonman
Mickson, Archibald	Soldier in Bn. of Minute Men
Middleton, Hatton	Captain in Bn. of Minute Men
Middleton, Robert	Appointed Captain in Bn. of Minute Men
Miller, Charles	Private in Bn. of Minute Men
Miller, Daniel	Refugee
Miller, Elisha	Captain in the Ga. Line
Miller, George	Soldier in Bn. of Minute Men
Miller, George Sr.	Soldier in Bn. of MInute Men
Miller, Moses	Refugee
Miller, Nathaniel	Refugee in Col. James McCay's Reg.
Miller, Nicholas	Refugee
Miller, Samuel	Soldier in Bn. of Minute Men
Miller, Samuel	"Mary Miller, relict and executrix of Samuel Miller, late of Sunbury (deceased) makes humble application to your honors for the Bounty lands due by law, to the legal representative of the said deceased, he having died in Refugeeship, and before his death, and as long as his health would premit being in the appointment of assistant Deputy Commissary of Purchases to the American Army as per certificate Colo. Carington here with prefixed. /S/ Mary Miller;" Samuel Miller was survived by wife, Mary, and a son, Morris who was an infant in March 1784
Miller, Smith	Soldier, Cont. Reg. of Light Horse, under command of Col. Leonard Marbury
Miller, William	Refugee
Miller, William	Soldier in Bn. of Minute Men
Mills, George	Refugee
Milner, John	Refugee from Wilkes Co., Ga.

Mitchell, David	Soldier in Col. Stewart's Bn. of Minute Men
Mitchell, John	"It appears by a Brevet under the hand of John Stirk, Esq., Colonel of the Third Ga. Continental Reg. that John Mitchell was appointed First Lieut. of the said Reg. the 5th. Day of April, 1778 and that he continued in service until sometime in the summer of 1782 . . . . /S/ Lach. McIntosh, Major General."
Mitchell, Robert	Refugee under command of Col. Elijah Clarke
Mitchell, William	Refugee
Mitchell, William	Cont. Soldier of Ga. Line
Mocock, Henry	Soldier, 1st. Bn. of Minute Men
Moffett, Thomas	Refugee
Montgomery, James	Refugee
Moore, Alexander	Refugee
Moore, John	Sergeant in Bn. of Minute Men
Moore, Richard	Private in Bn. of Minute Men
Moore, Stephen	"I do certify that Stephen Moore was a Sergeant in the Regiment under my command and that he lost his life in the service of his country. /S/ Leonard Marbury, Lt. Col.;" Stephen Moore was survived by wife, Mary Moore
Moore, William	Refugee
Moore, William	Private in Bn. of Minute Men
Morgan, Christopher	Private, Captain Shem Thomson's Co., Col. Samuel Jack's Bn. of Minute Men
Morgan, Jeremiah	Refugee
Morgan, Jesse	"This is to certify that Jesey Morgan was one of those worthy citizens that fled British protection and took refuge in the other states and faithfully did his duty as a good soldier until he got wounded in defence of this state at the first siege of Au-

gusta. He afterwards joined Col. Clarke when he returned to this state and was part of the time with Capt. Dunn before the Battle of Long Cane and is entitled to land as a refugee. /S/ William Candler, Colo of the Regent, R.R.C."

Morgan, John	Refugee; was living in Meeklenburg Co., Virginia in February 1784
Morgan, Malachiah	Refugee
Morgan, Philip	Soldier, 3rd. Ga. Cont. Bn. under command of Captain Isaac Hicks; Morgan lived in Meeklenburg Co., Virginia when discharged on December 23, 1782; he had served for three years
Morphet, Thomas	Refugee
Morris, James	Soldier, 1st. Bn. of Minute Men
Morris, Patrick	Soldier in Bn. of Minute Men; was in the siege of Augusta
Morris, William	Sergeant in Bn. of Minute Men
Morrison, John	Captain in Ga. State Legion under command of Lt. Col. James Jackson
Mosby, Littleberry	Captain
Mosby, Robert	Lt., Ga. Cont. Line from August 1776 to November 1779
Mosely, Jesse	Soldier, Light Dragoons for the State of Ga., commanded by Col. Leonard Marbury; Mosely enlisted by Captain Cade for eighteen months and discharged on February 13, 1778
Mosely, John	Soldier, Light Dragoons for the State of Ga., commanded by Col. Leonard Marbury; Mosely enlisted by Captain Cade for eighteen months and discharged on February 13, 1778
Mosely, William	Refugee
Moss, Leonard	Served in Ga. State Legion under command of Lt. Col. James Jackson

Mumford, Thomas	Soldier, Ga. Cont. Line
Murphy, Mills	Refugee in North Carolina
Musteen, William	Private, 3rd. Ga. Bn.; was a prisoner for a time
Myers, Thomas	Served for three years as a Private on board one of the state's galleys
Nail, Benjamin	Refugee Sergeant
Nail, Henry	Refugee
Nail, John	Soldier in Bn. of Minute Men
Nail, Joseph	Refugee Soldier
Nail, Joseph	Captain in Bn. of Refugees
Nail, Reuben	Refugee
Nash, Clement	Captain; deceased prior to May 1784; survived by wife, Mary Nash
Neal, Patrick	Soldier of the Ga. Line
Neidlinger, John Godleib	Refugee under command of Jenkins Davis
Neilly, John	Private in Bn. of Minute Men
Nelson, James	Private in Bn. of Minute Men
Nelson, John	Refugee
Nelson, William	Soldier in Reg. under command of Col. Leonard Marbury
Nelson, William	Soldier, 1st. Bn. of Minute Men
Nephew, James	Refugee
Nesler, Adam	Refugee
Nettles, Elisha	Soldier, 1st. Bn. of Minute Men
Nevill, Thomas	Soldier in Bn. of Minute Men
Newly, Peter	Soldier in Bn. of Minute Men
Newman, John	Soldier, 2nd. Ga. Cont. Reg., Ga. Line; had his arm shot off while in the service
Newman, William	Private in Bn. of Minute Men
Nicholson, Benjamin	Soldier in Bn. of Minute Men
Nickson, Archable	Soldier in Bn. of Minute Men
Nivel, Peter	Soldier in Bn. of Minute Men
Nix, George	Private, 2nd. Ga. Line; served three years
Nixon, Solomon	Soldier in Bn. of Minute Men
Nixon, Solomon	Soldier in Reg. under command of Col. Leonard Marbury

Nobles, Merideth	Soldier in Bn. of Minute Men
Norwood, Richard	Soldier in Bn. of Minute Men
Nugan, Michael	Private, 2nd. Ga. Cont. Bn.
Oakman, William	Fife Major, 2nd. Ga. Cont. Reg.
O'Barn, William	Soldier in Bn. of Minute Men
O'Bryan, James	Private, 3rd. Ga. Bn.
O'Bryant, Dunkin	Soldier in Bn. of Minute Men
Odier, William	Soldier in Bn. of Minute Men
Odingsells, Charles	Served under command of Brig. Gen. Marion
Odom, Uriah	Soldier, 1st. Bn. of Minute Men
Offutt, Ezekiel	Refugee Captain under command of Col. William Candler
Offutt, Jesse	Refugee under command of Col. William Candler at the first siege of Augusta
Offutt, Nathaniel	Refugee under command of Col. William Candler
O'Hearn, Josiah	Refugee in North Carolina
O'Neal, William	Refugee
O'Neally, Abraham	Soldier in Bn. of Minute Men
Onslow, George	Soldier in Bn. of Minute Men
Ornsby, Daniel	"This certifys that Daniel Ornsby, Fife Major, in the first Company, of the 2nd. Georgia Contl. Battalion, was enlisted for the term of three years and that he died in the said service, and that Mary Berry (at present so called) was his wife at the time and before his death. I further certify that the said Daniel Ornsbe left a daughter (called Isabella) which is now alive, and with the mother Mary Berry. Given under my hand at Augusta the 10th. Day of April, 1784. /S/ J. Pannill, Lt. Col."
Orvie, James	Served in the Revolution
Osgood, John	Refugee
Outlaw, Edward	Refugee
Outlaw, Lodwick	"This is to certify that Lodwick Outlaw

	served as a faithful refugee and served after the reduction of Augusta as a good soldier until the first of March following on his way to Savannah took sick and died is left behind him one son named James Outlaw.... Given under my hand this 16 day of February, 1784. /S/ John Twiggs, B.G."
Owens, Aaron	Soldier in Reg. under command of Col. Leonard Marbury
Owens, Robert	Refugee
Owsley, Abraham	Soldier in Bn. of Minute Men
Pace, Thomas	Refugee; "I hereby certify that Mr. Thomas Pace was taken prisoner by the enemy the British at the time of Col. Clarkes first siege at Augusta and sent to Charles Town and kept there as such until he the said Pace broke costody and made his escape back and joined the Georgia Refugees before the fall of Augusta. Certified by me this 26th. day of July, 1784. /S/ James Martin, Col."
Pace, Thomas	Refugee under command of Col. James Martin and Militia Soldier under command of Col. James McNeal
Paine, Samuel	Soldier in Bn. of Minute Men
Paine, Samuel	Private in Bn. of Minute Men
Palmer, John	Refugee
Palmer, John	Soldier in Bn. of Minute Men
Palmer, John	Quartermaster under command of Major Francis Boykin
Pannill, Joseph	"This certifys that Joseph Pannill, Esquire, was appointed a Captain in the Second Georgia Continental Regiment the 20th. of August, 1778, and a Major in the same Regiment the 17th. September, 1777 and a Lieutenant Colonel in the Forth

	Georgia Regiment the 27th. May, 1778 and continued in service until he was deranged by Resolve of Congress the 3rd. and 21. October, 1780. Given under my hand at Savannah, the 1st. February, 1784. /S/ Lachn. McIntosh, Major General."
Parham, Richard	Soldier, Captain Isaac Hick's Co., 3rd. Ga. Cont. Bn.; Parham formerly resided in Warren Co., North Carolina; he died while in service
Parker, James	Soldier, Ga. Cont. Line
Parker, John	Refugee Lt.
Parker, John	Soldier, Ga. Cont. Line
Parks, John	Lt.
Parmer, Solomon	Soldier
Partin, John	Refugee
Paskin, Hugh	Soldier in Bn. of Minute Men
Patterson, Gideon	Lt. in Captain Hezekiah Wade's Co., Col. Samuel Jack's Bn. of Minute Men; went on Florida expedition
Patterson, Gideon	Refugee
Patterson, John	Refugee
Patterson, John Jr.	Refugee; was residing in Burke Co., Ga. in January 1784
Patterson, Robert	Refugee in North Carolina
Pattillo, John	Soldier, 3rd. Ga. Cont. Reg.; was deceased prior to December 1784, leaving heir James Pattillo of Brunswick Co., Virginia
Paulk, Micajah	Served in the Revolution
Paxton, William	Lt. in Bn. of Minute Men
Paxton, William	Sergeant, Light Dragoons, Cont. Reg., under command of Lt. Col. Leonard Marbury; Paxton was deceased prior to April 1785; he was survived by widow, Mary Hooper
Payne, Thomas	Lt.

Peal, John	Refugee
Pearce, Jesse	Soldier, 1st. Bn. of Minute Men
Pearce, John	Soldier, 1st. Bn. of Minute Men
Pearce, William	Soldier, 1st. Bn. of Minute Men
Pearre, Nathanial	Lt. Cont. Line
Peavy, Abraham	Militia Private
Peavy, John	Served in the Revolution
Peavy, Peter	Militia Soldier
Peek, John	Served in the Revolution
Perkins, Benjamin	Soldier in Bn. of Minute Men
Perkins, Efram	Soldier in Bn. of Minute Men
Perkins, Isaac	Soldier in Bn. of Minute Men
Perritt, Robert	Soldier in Bn. of Minute Men
Persett, John	Refugee
Persons, Jones	Refugee
Peteet, Benjamin	"I swear to be true to the State of Georgia, and to serve it honestly and faithfully, in the Battalion commanded by Col. John Stuart against all enemies whatsoever, and to observe and obey the Orders of the Assembly of this State, and those of the Generals and Officers set over me by them; and I do further swear that I do not belong to any other regular Regiment in the Service of this or any other of the United States of America; that I am by trade a talor and to the best of my information and belief was born in the County of Pyerdy, in France and that I have no Rupture, nor are troubled with Fits; that I am no way disabled bu Main or otherwise that will prevent my discharging the duty of a Soldier, and that I voluntarily enlist myself in the service of the State of Georgia as a Soldier to serve during the Space of two years after being embodied in this State unless sooner discharged and I have

received the Sum of thirty two dollars enlisting money, and that I will lay down my arms peacable when required by the Assembly or Executive Powers of this State. Sworn to before me, one of the Justices of the Peace for the County of Wilkes in the State of Georgia this 16th Day of August, 1777. /S/ John Burks. The abovementioned Benjamin Petite is aged forty-five years, five Feet, five Inches high, of a Dark complexion, black Hair, black Eyes, well made." "This is to certify that the bearer Benjamin Petee a private in Captain John Burke's Company of Minute Men commanded by Col. John Stuart is hereby discharged from the service of this state. Given under my hand this 27th. of July, 1778. /S/ Elijah Clark, Col."

Peters, Isaac	Soldier in Bn. of Minute Men
Peters, John	Soldier in Bn. of Minute Men
Peters, Jonathan	Refugee
Peters, Solomon	Soldier in Bn. of Minute Men
Peterson, James	Soldier, Ga. Cont. Line
Peterson, John	Soldier in Bn. of Minute Men
Peterson, John	Soldier, Ga. Cont. Line
Peterson, William	Soldier, Ga. Cont. Line
Pettit, Benjamin	"By Colonel Joseph Habersham, of the First Battalion of Continental Troops of Georgia, in the Service of the United States of America. These are to certify, That the Bearer hereof Benjn. Pettit, a private soldier, has served in the above Regiment, and in Captain John Habersham's Company, for the space of twelve Months, for which Term he inlisted, and is hereby discharged from the said Regiment, he having received his Pay, Arrears of Pay,

	Cloathins, and all other just demands, from the Time of his inlisting in the said Regiment, to this day of Discharge, as appears by his Receipt on the Back hereof. Given under my hand, and the Seal of the Battalion, at Savannah, this 22nd. Day of May, 1777. /S/ Jo. Habersham."
Petty, William	Private, 1st. Bn. of Minute Men
Phelps, David	Sergeant in Bn. of Minute Men
Phelps. David	Refugee Lt.
Pheny, Lacklin	Refugee in South Carolina
Pheny, Lacklin	Private, 2nd. Ga. Cont. Reg., Captain William Lane's Co.; was recruited in Virginia for defence of Ga.; was made a prisoner at the reduction of Savannah
Phillips, David	Refugee Lt.
Phillips, Joel	Refugee
Phillips, Joel Jr.	Refugee
Phillips. John	Soldier in Bn. of Minute Men
Phillips, Joseph	Was in the Minute Service; died while in service; survived by wife (and widow) Casander Phillips and one son, Isom Phillips
Phillips, Joseph	Refugee
Phillips, Joseph Jr.	Refugee
Phillips, Joshua Jr.	Refugee
Phillips, Mark	Refugee
Phillips, Reubin	Refugee
Phillips, William	Refugee
Phillips, Zachary	Refugee
Phillips, Zachary	Refugee Captain
Pinkins, Benjamin	Soldier in Bn. of Minute Men
Platen, Benjamin	Soldier in Bn. of Minute Men
Plummer, Joseph	Refugee
Polk, John	Served in the Revolution
Pollard, Demey	Soldier in Bn. of Minute Men
Porter, Benjamin	Major, 2nd. Ga. Cont. Bn.

Porter, Josiah	Soldier, Captain Michael Dickson's Co., Col. Samuel Jack's Bn. of Minute Men
Porter, Sampson	Soldier in Bn. of Minute Men
Porter, Thomas	Lt.
Porter, Thomas	Captain
Porterus, Simon	Soldier in Bn. of Minute Men
Pothill, Jeremiah	Soldier in Bn. of Minute Men
Potts, John	Private in Bn. of Minute Men
Pound, Reuben	Private in 2nd. Ga. Bn.; served for three years
Pounds, Samuel	Refugee
Powell, Benjamin	Soldier in Bn. of Minute Men
Powell, James	Refugee; was a prisoner for a considerable time
Powell, Joshua	Soldier in Bn. of Minute Men
Powell, Josiah	Refugee
Powell, Lewis	Soldier in Bn. of Minute Men commanded by Col. Elijah Clark
Powers, David	Soldier in Bn. of Minute Men
Powers, John	Soldier in Bn. of Minute Men
Pray, Job	Captain
Price, John	First Lt., Wilkes Co. Reg. of Refugees
Pugh, James Jr.	Refugee
Pulliam, William	Refugee
Purkins, Benjamin	Soldier in Bn. of Minute Men
Pusley, David	Soldier
Quarterman, William	Refugee
Queen, William	Soldier
Rae, James	Deputy Commissary General of Purchases of Ga. from sometime in 1776 until February 1780; was in the State and Continental service
Rafferty, Michael	Refugee under command of Col. Elijah Clarke
Ragland, Benjamin	Refugee under command of Col. Elijah Clarke
Ragland, Evan	Refugee Lt.

Ramsey, Isaac Jr.	Soldier in Bn. of Minute Men
Ramsey, Isaac Sr.	Soldier in Bn. of Minute Men
Ramsey, John Sr.	Soldier, 1st. Bn. of Minute Men
Ramsey, Randal	Soldier, Captain Chessley Bostwick's Co., 1st. Ga. Bn. of Cont. Troops
Ramsey, Samuel	Soldier in Ga. State Legion under command of Lt. Col. James Jackson; Ramsey was killed while in service; he was a brother to John Ramsey
Ramsey, Thomas	Soldier in Bn. of Minute Men
Randal, Obadiah	Soldier, Cont. Light Horse of Ga.
Raser, Isaac	Refugee
Ratcliff, James	Soldier in Bn. of Minute Men
Ray, Ambrose	Refugee
Ray, William	Soldier in Ga. State Legion under command of Lt. Col. James Jackson
Read, William Dr.	"This certifys that William Reed, Esquire, was appointed Second Surgeon of the General Hospital in the Middle District the 9th. July, 1778, was promoted to be Hospital Physician the 15th. May, 1781 and continued to serve in that capacity to the end of the War. Given under my hand at Savannah the 26th. Feb., 1784. /S/ Lackn. McIntosh, Maj. Gen."
Reaves, James	Soldier in Bn. of Minute Men
Red, Henry	Soldier, Ga. Cont. Line
Red, John	Soldier in Bn. of Minute Men
Red, Peter	Soldier in Bn. of Minute Men
Redman, William	Soldier, Ga. Cont. Line
Reed, Thomas	Soldier, Ga. Cont. Line
Reeder, James	Soldier, Ga. Cont. Line
Reeder, William	Soldier, Ga. Cont. Line
Rees, David	Deputy Judge Advocate in the American Army
Reese, Jonathan	Soldier in Bn. of Minute Men
Reeves, David	Corporal in Bn. of Minute Men

Reeves, David	Soldier in Bn. of Minute Men
Reeves, Davis	Soldier in Reg. under command of Col. Leonard Marbury
Rench, John	Soldier in Bn. of Minute Men
Reyfield, Isaac	Soldier, 2nd. Bn. Cont Troops; enlisted for three years; was killed while in service
Reynolds, Absolom	"State of Georgia. Absolom Reynolds a Fifer in the 3rd. Company of the Second Georgia Continental Regiment, being sworn upon the Holy Evangelist of Almighty God maketh oath that he was inlisted in the room of John Boling of said Regiment, he being very sickly. This deponent took his place for eighteen months and a half from the 13th day of February, 1778 and approved of by Colonel Elbert of the same Regt. This deponent further saith that John Boling has six months pay due him as a Private soldier in the said Regt. viz. the months of September, October, November, & December, 1777, January & February, 1778. And that the said John Boling gave an order to this deponent to receive it as a bounty for supplying his place and that this deponent has the months of July & August, 1779 due him. Absalom Reynolds, his X mark." "Absolom Reynolds, Fifer in the Second Georgia Contl. Regiment is hereby discharged the service. He having served his country faithfully during the time of his inlistment.... Given under my hand at Head Quarters, Augusta in Georgia this 3rd. Sept., 1779. /S/ Lachn McIntosh, Br. Gen."
Rheny, William	Militia Soldier
Rice, John	Soldier in Bn. of Minute Men

Rice, Nathan	Soldier in Bn. of Minute Men
Rice, Peter	Soldier in Bn. of Minute Men
Rice, Peter	Soldier in Bn. of Minute Men
Richards, Jacob	Soldier in Bn. of Minute Men
Richie, John	Lt. in Bn. of Minute Men
Riddle, William	Private in Bn. of Minute Men
Riden, Joseph Scott	Refugee under command of Col. Elijah Clark
Rider, Isaac	Soldier in Bn. of Minute Men
Rider, Jacob	Soldier in Bn. of Minute Men
Rider, Peter	Soldier in Bn. of Minute Men
Rider, William	Soldier, Ga. Cont. Line
Riding, George	Refugee
Roan, Tudstall	Militia Soldier in John Antony's Co.
Roberson, Alexander	Private, 3rd. Ga. Reg.
Roberson, David	Soldier in Bn. of Minute Men
Roberts, Absalom	Soldier in Col. Leonard Marbury's Reg.
Roberts, Francis	Soldier, 1st. Bn. of Minute Men
Roberts, Harris	Soldier in Bn. of Minute Men
Roberts, James	Refugee
Roberts, John	Refugee
Roberts, John	Soldier in Bn. of Minute Men
Robertson, Joseph	Private, Captain Michal Dickson's Co., Col. Samuel Jack's Bn. of Minute Men
Robertson, Zadock	Private, 1st. Bn. of Minute Men
Robeson, David	Refugee Lt. Col.
Robeson, Jonathan	Refugee who "fell glorously fighting for the same (United States)"
Robinson, David	Soldier in Bn. of Minute Men
Robinson, William	Soldier in Reg. of Dragoons
Rock, James	Soldier in Bn. of Minute Men
Rodgers, Jese	Soldier in Bn. of Minute Men
Rodgers, John	Soldier in Bn. of Minute Men
Rodgers, Peter	Soldier in Bn. of Minute Men
Rodgers, Solomon	Soldier in Bn. of Minute Men
Roe, James	Refugee under command of Col. William Candler

Roe, Robert	Soldier in Reg. under command of Col. Leonard Marbury
Roe, Walter	Soldier in Bn. of Minute Men
Rogan, Felix	Refugee
Roger, Jacob	Soldier in Bn. of Minute Men
Rogers, Britain	Refugee
Rogers, Dread	Refugee
Rogers, Edward	Soldier, Ga. Cont. Line
Rogers, Edward	Private in Bn. of Minute Men
Rogers, John	Refugee
Rogers, Peter	Soldier in Reg. under command of Col. Leonard Marbury
Rogers, Thomas	Soldier, Ga. Cont. Line
Rogers, William	Refugee
Rogers, William	Sergeant in Bn. of Minute Men
Roling, John	Soldier in Bn. of Minute Men
Rollins, Barnard	Soldier in Bn. of Minute Men
Rollins, David	Soldier in Bn. of Minute Men
Rollins, John Jr.	Soldier in Bn. of Minute Men
Rollins, John Sr.	Soldier in Bn. of Minute Men
Roquemore, Peter	Refugee Lt.
Rose, John	Refugee
Rose, Walton	Soldier in Bn. of Minute Men
Roseborough, George	Soldier; was killed in service
Roundtree, Abner	Refugee; joined Col. William Candler's Reg. at the 1st. Siege of Augusta
Roundtree, Jesse	Refugee; joined Col. William Candler's Reg. at the 1st. siege of Augusta
Roundtree, Jobe	Refugee; joined Col. William Candler's Reg. at the 1st. siege of Augusta
Rowlan, Dyal	Refugee
Rowland, Samuel	Private in Bn. of Minute Men
Rowley, John	Soldier in Bn. of Minute Men
Rowling, David	Soldier in Bn. of Minute Men
Rowling, John	Soldier in Bn. of Minute Men
Rowling, John Jr.	Soldier in Bn. of Minute Men
Rozer, Amos	Soldier in Bn. of Minute Men

Rozer, Caleb	Refugee
Runnalds, George	Soldier
Runnalds, George	Soldier in Bn. of Minute Men
Runnalds, Hambleton	Soldier
Runnels, Coleman	Refugee
Ruroy, James	Soldier in Bn. of Minute Men
Rushing, Matthew	Refugee
Russell, William	Soldier in Bn. of Minute Men
Ryall, Richard	Soldier in Reg. under command of Col. Leonard Marbury
Ryan, James	Soldier in Bn. of Minute Men
Ryley, Barnard	Soldier in Bn. of Minute Men
Ryley, John	Soldier in Bn. of Minute Men
Rynan, George	Soldier in Reg. of Dragoons
Salisberry, Thomas	Soldier, 2nd. Ga. Bn., commanded by Col. Jo. Elburt
Sallet, Robert	Refugee
Salter, Simon	Soldier, Captain Henry Duke's Co., Col. Samuel Jack's Bn. of Minute Men
Sanders, John	Soldier in Reg. under command of Col. Leonard Marbury
Sanders, John	Refugee
Sanders, Simon	Soldier in Bn. of Minute Men
Savage, Loveless, Rev.	Refugee Chaplain
Scott, Alexander, Rev.	Chaplain, Effingham Co., Militia
Scott, Alexander	Soldier, Reg. of Cont. Light Dragoons under command of Lt. Col. Leonard Marbury
Scott, Cornelius	Soldier in Bn. of Minute Men
Scott, John	Soldier in Bn. of Minute Men
Scott, John Jr.	Soldier, 1st. Bn. of Minute Men
Scott, John Sr.	Soldier, 1st. Bn. of Minute Men
Scott, Joseph	Soldier
Scott, Peter	Sergeant in Bn. of Minute Men
Scott, William	Appointed Captain in the Ga. Cont. Line in 1777
Scott, William	Soldier in Bn. of Minute Men

Scott, William Jr.	Soldier, 1st. Bn. of Minute Men
Sessoms, William Jr.	"State of Georgia, Wilkes County. We do certify that William Sessoms, Junior, was inlisted for three years under Captain John Dooly in the Third Battallion of Foot, commanded by Colo. James Scriven as a private, and behaved himself as a good soldier. Given under our hands this 21st. May, 1784. /S/ Thomas Mitchell, 1st. Lt. /S/ George Dooly, 2nd. Lt."
Shackleford, John	Refugee
Shaddock, Thomas	Refugee
Sharpe, James Boyd, Dr.	"Savannah, 18th. March, 1784. This is to certify that there being no person to act as Surgeon to the late Georgia Battalion, I appointed Mr. James B. Sharpe to do that duty on the 6t. December, 1782; and as he continued to serve in that capacity till the War terminated, I think him entitled to the pay and emoluments of a Surgeon's Mate, as the Battalion consisted only of three Companies, and consequently a full Surgeon could not be appointed to it. /S/ John Habersham, Major Commt., late Geoa. Batt."
Shaw, David	Soldier in Bn. of Minute Men
Shaw, Thomas Jr.	Private, 1st. Bn. of Minute Men
Shaw, Thomas Sr.	Sergeant, 1st. Bn. of Minute Men
Sheffel, Mark	Refugee
Sheffel, William	Refugee
Shepheard, Stephen	Soldier in Bn. of Minute Men
Sherman, John	Soldier in Bn. of Minute Men
Sherril, David	Refugee
Shick, Frederick	Lt. in the Ga. Cont. Line
Shields, Andrew	Refugee and Private Soldier in the 1st. Ga., Bn., Cont. Troops
Shields, John	Refugee Major; "State of Georgia, Rich-

mond County. This is to certify that Maj. John Shields was one of those worthy Citizens that Fled British protenction, and joined me the first Siege of Augusta, and faithfully did duty as a good Soldier, and Gloriously lost his Life fighting for the State, and is intitled to every Bounty Due to his rank. Certifyd, by William Candler, Col."

Shields, William	Refugee
Shirley, John	Private in Col. Samuel Jack's Bn. of Minute Men
Shiver, Robert	Soldier in Reg. under command of Col. Leonard Marbury
Shomaker, David	Refugee
Showers, David	Soldier in Bn. of Minute Men
Showers, Peter	Soldier in Bn. of Minute Men
Simmons, Charles	Refugee
Simmons, James	Soldier in Bn. of Minute Men
Simmons, James	Refugee
Simmons, Richard	Soldier in Bn. of Minute Men
Simmons, Thomas	Soldier in Bn. of Minute Men
Simons, Richard	Soldier in Reg. under command of Col. Leonard Marbury
Simpson, James	Served in the Revolution
Simpson, Samuel	Soldier
Sims, Mann	Soldier
Sims, Robert	Soldier, 2nd. Ga. Bn.
Sims, Thomas	Soldier in Reg. of Dragoons
Sinquefield, Samuel	Refugee
Sinquefield, William	Soldier in Bn. of Minute Men
Sizemore, Isaac	Soldier in Bn. of Minute Men
Sizemore, William	Soldier in Bn. of Minute Men
Skinner, Isaac	Refugee Captain
Slecker, George	Soldier in Col. Stuart's Bn. of Minute Men; was residing in Camden District, South Carolina in April 1784

Slocum, Seth	Refugee in North Carolina; was killed while in service
Smart, Robert	Private in Bn. of Minute Men
Smith, Abraham	Private, 1st. Bn. of Minute Men
Smith, Arthur	Refugee
Smith, Burrell	Refugee
Smith, Cornelius	Refugee
Smith, Ebenezer	Refugee
Smith, Jacob	Soldier in Captain John Awtry's Co.; was taken prisoner during the siege of Augusta
Smith, James	Refugee
Smith, John	Soldier in Bn. of Minute Men
Smith, John	Soldier in Captain Richard Austin's Co. of Minute Men
Smith, Moses	Soldier in Bn. of Minute Men
Smith, Nathan	Refugee
Smith, Nathaniel	Refugee
Smith, Peter	Soldier in Bn. of Minute Men
Smith, Samuel	Refugee
Smith, Simon	Sergeant in Bn. of Minute Men
Smith, Thomas	Drummer in Bn. of Minute Men
Smith, Thomas	Soldier in Bn. of Minute Men
Smith, Thomas	Refugee
Smith, Thomas Jr.	Refugee
Sneed, Dudley	Refugee under command of Col. Elijah Clarke
Snelson, Thomas Jr.	Sergeant in Bn. of Minute Men
Soulter, John	Soldier in Bn. of Minute Men
Southerland, John	Soldier in Reg. under command of Col. Leonard Marbury
Southerland, Thomas	Soldier in Bn. of Minute Men
Spencer, William	Refugee
Spikes, Elias	Soldier in Bn. of Minute Men
Spikes, Joseph	Soldier, Ga. Cont. Line
Spurlock, Robert	Refugee Private; was deceased prior to May 1784
Stallings, Ezekiel	Refugee under command of Col. William

Stallings, Frederick	Refugee Captain in Reg. under command of Col. William Candler; was killed by the enemy
Stallings, James	Refugee Lt. under command of Col. William Candler
Stallings, Jesse	Militia Soldier in Captain Heard's Co.
Stallings, John	Refugee
Stanley, James	Killed by the enemy while in the service of the state; survived by wife. Mary, and two children
Statt, John	Soldier in Bn. of Minute Men
Statt, Peter	Soldier in Bn. of Minute Men
Stedham, John	Soldier in Bn. of Minute Men
Steed, Edward	Soldier in Bn. of Minute Men
Steed, Phillip	Soldier in Bn. of Minute Men and Militia Soldier
Steed, Phillip	Private, 1st. Bn. of Minute Men
Steele, Nicholous	Soldier in Bn. of Minute Men
Stephens, Benjamin	Soldier in Bn. of Minute Men
Stephens, John	Soldier, 2nd. Ga. Bn.
Stephens, Thomas	Soldier in Bn. of Minute Men
Stevens, John	Refugee
Stewart, Charles	Lt. in Captain Walker's Co., Col. John Stewart's Bn. of Minute Men
Stewart, James	Refugee
Stewart, James	Adjutant of the 1st. Bn. of Minute Men
Stewart, James Sr.	Refugee
Stewart, John	Col. of a Bn. of Minute Men
Stewart, John	Refugee; was killed while in service
Stewart, Samuel	Soldier in Bn. of Minute Men
Still, Joseph	"The petition of Joseph Still Showeth that your petitioner was taken prisoner in Sunbury and put on board a prison ship. That after his release from thence he did Militia duty under Colo. Cooper in Liberty County and with Colo. Jackson below

	Ebenezer. He therefore prays your honors to grant him a warrant for his Refugee Rights. Oct. 3, 1785. /S/ Joseph Still."
Stockham, Seth	Soldier in Bn. of Minute Men
Stockwell, Thomas	Soldier in Bn. of Minute Men
Stone, Charles	Private in Bn. of Minute Men
Stone, Joshua	Soldier in Bn. of Minute Men
Stout, David	Soldier in Bn. of Minute Men
Stram, James	Soldier in Bn. of Minute Men
Strange, Ephram	Soldier, Cont. Light Horse of Ga.
Strange, John	Soldier in Bn. of Minute Men
Stringer, John	Soldier in Bn. of Minute Men
Strohaker, Rudolph	Refugee under command of Gen. Lincoln and other officers
Strosier, Peter	Refugee
Stuart, Clement	Soldier, 1st. Bn. of Minute Men
Stuart, David	Soldier in Bn. of Minute Men
Stuart, John	Refugee; was deceased prior to May 1784
Stuart, Samuel	Soldier, 1st. Bn. of Minute Men
Studstill, John	Soldier in Bn. of Minute Men
Stumps, Peter	Soldier in Reg. under command of Col. Leonard Marbury
Sullers, Samuel	Soldier in Reg. under command of Col. Leonard Marbury
Sullivan, Owen	Soldier in Bn. of Minute Men
Sullivan, William	Refugee
Sullivant, William	Refugee
Sullivant, William	Soldier in Bn. of Minute Men
Summerford, Jacob	Soldier in Bn. of Minute Men commanded by Col. Elijah Clarke
Summerford, Jacob Jr.	Soldier in Bn. of Minute Men
Summerford, Richard	Soldier in Bn. of Minute Men commanded by Col. Elijah Clarke
Summerlin, James	Refugee
Summers, Demsey	Soldier in Bn. of Minute Men
Summers, Denney	Soldier in Bn. of Minute Men
Summers, John	Soldier in Bn. of Minute Men

Summers, Samuel	Soldier in Bn. of Minute Men
Sumner, Solomon	Soldier in Bn. of Minute Men
Sures, John	Soldier in Bn. of Minute Men
Sutherlin, Thomas	Private in Bn. of Minute Men
Sutton, Ralph	"These are to certify that Ralph Sutton enlisted in the Georgia First Battalion of Infantry and served one year being the time of his enlistment. Given under my hand this 12 March, 1784. /S/ Igns. Few, Captain." "This is to certify that to the best of my remenbrance Corporal Ralph Sutton was reenlisted to serve in the Continental Army during the War, and that he was made prisoner by the British Troops when they took Savannah, in December, 1778. I am informed he afterwards died on board one of their prison ships. Savannah, 24th. March, 1784. /S/ John Habersham, Major, late Geoa. Line." Ralph Sutton was survived by wife, Winney Sutton
Swords, James	Soldier, 1st. Bn. of Minute Men
Sykes, Daniel	Refugee
Tannyhill, John	Private in Bn. of Minute Men
Taylor, James	Captain in Bn. of Minute Men
Taylor, Randolph	Refugee
Tennille, Francis	Captain
Thegott, John	Soldier in Bn. of Minute Men
Thomas, Benjamin	Soldier in Bn. of Minute Men
Thomas, Benjamin	Sergeant, Light Dragoons of the Ga. Cont. Line
Thomas, James	Soldier, 1st. Bn. of Minute Men
Thomas, Jese	Soldier in Bn. of Minute Men
Thomas, Peter	Refugee
Thomas, Samuel	Refugee
Thompson, Benjamin	Refugee
Thompson, Benjamin Jr.	Refugee
Thompson, Drury	Refugee

Thompson, Isham	Refugee
Thompson, James	Refugee
Thompson, James	Soldier in Ga. Cont. Troop of Horse under command of Col. Baker
Thompson, Jesse	Soldier in Bn. of Minute Men; was on Florida expedition
Thompson, John	Refugee Captain
Thompson, John Farley	Refugee under comand of Col. Elijah Clarke
Thompson, Robert	Refugee
Thompson, William	Soldier, 3rd. Reg., Ga. Cont. Troops
Thompson, William	Refugee
Thompson, William Jr.	Soldier, 3rd. Reg., Ga. Cont. Troops
Thorn, David	Militia Soldier under command of Col. Caleb Howell; Thorn served from February 1782 until the exclusion of the enemy from Savannah
Thorn, William	Militia Soldier and Refugee; while a Refugee he was under the command of several officers including Col. Jenkins Davis, from 1778 to 1782
Thorpe, John	Refugee
Threadgill, Thomas	Captain
Thurman, John	Refugee
Tindall, William	Served in the Revolution
Tomlinson, David	Soldier, Captain William Ames' Co., Col. Stewart's Bn., later Col. Elijah Clark's Bn. of Minute Men; Tomlinson was in the Florida expedition and was discharged by Col. Clarke at Midway when they returned from Florida
Tompson, William	Refugee
Torrence, John	Refugee under command of Col. William Candler
Towns, John	Private in Bn. of Minute Men
Trammell, Dennis	Refugee
Trapp, Joseph	Militia Soldier and Soldier in Bn. of Min-

	ute Men
Traywick, Francis	Was wounded in the service of Ga. whereby he was rendered incapable of supporting himself and family
Troy, John	Soldier, Cont. Reg. of Light Dragoons under command of Col. Leonard Marbury
Troy, John	Soldier in Bn. of Minute Men
Troy, John	Soldier in Bn. of Minute Men
Troy, John	Refugee
Tucker, George	Refugee
Tucker, Paschal	Private, 3rd. Ga. Bn.
Tucker, Thomas	Soldier in Bn. of Minute Men
Tucker, Thomas Jr.	Refugee
Tully, William	Refugee
Tunus, Nehemiah	Sergeant in Bn. of Minute Men
Turner, Charles	"Brunswick County, Virginia, January 27th., 1784. This is to certify that Charles Turner of Muhlenburg County, Virginia, enlisted as a soldier in my Company to serve three years in the Continental Army and that he died while in the said service. Given under my hand the day and date above written. /S/ Isaac Hicks, Capt., 3d. Georgia Contn Batt."
Turner, David	"I hereby certify that David Turner was Captain-Lieutenant of Captain Thomas Morris's Company of (Georgia Cont.) Artillery, and continued in the service of the United States of America until (as I am informed) he died in December, 1778. Given at Savannah, 9th. March, 1784. /S/ John Habersham, Major of the late Geo. Line."
Turner, Dennis	Soldier in Cont. Reg. of Light Horse of State of Ga. under command of Col. Leonard Marbury
Turner, George	Soldier, 3rd. Bn. of Ga. Cont. Line

Turner, Henry	Soldier in Bn. of Minute Men
Turner, John	Soldier in Bn. of Minute Men
Turner, John	Refugee
Turner, Peter	Soldier in Cont. Reg. of Light Horse of State of Ga. under command of Col. Leonard Marbury
Turner, Solomon	Soldier in Bn. of Minute Men
Turner, Thomas Jr.	Soldier in Cont. Reg. of Light Horse of State of Ga. under command of Col. Leonard Marbury
Turner, Thomas Sr.	Soldier in Cont. Reg. of Light Horse of State of Ga. under command of Col. Leonard Marbury
Tweedle, John	Sergeant, 1st. Ga. Cont. Bn.
Twiggs, John	Brigadier General
Van, Fur	Soldier in Bn. of Minute Men
Van, John	Soldier in Bn. of Minute Men
Van, Peter	Soldier in Bn. of Minute Men
Vanderherst, Jese	Soldier in Bn. of Minute Men
Vann, Cader	Soldier in Bn. of Minute Men
Vann, John	Refugee
Vann, Peter	Refugee
Vann, Ralph	Soldier in Bn. of Minute Men
Vickers, Solomon	"State of Georgia. I hereby certify that Solomon Vickers enlisted in the First Battalion of Continental Troops of the State of Georgia for one year after reenlisted to serve during the contest between Britian and America and died in the service. Certified by me. /S/ Igns. Few, Captain, Cont. Line."
Wade, Hezekiah	Captain in Bn. of Minute Men
Wade, John	Refugee in Reg. under command of Col. William Candler
Wade, Nathaniel	Refugee in Reg. under command of Col. William Candler
Wade, Nehemiah	Refugee in Reg. under command of Col.

	William Candler
Wagnon, Thomas	Soldier, 3rd. Ga. Cont. Reg.; enlisted in January 1777 for three years
Waldhauer, Jacob	"These are to certify that Mr. Jacob Waldhaur has supplyed the detachment under my command in going to Savanna with meat and drink for the sum of eleven shilling sterling. Witness this day of January, 1776. /S/ Thos. Chisolm (Captain). To the honourable Council of Safety in Savannah. Received the above eleven shillings this 29th. day, January, 1776 by me /S/ Jacob Waldhouer."
Walicon, Daniel Sr.	Refugee; was a prisoner at Charleston
Walker, Benjamin	Refugee
Walker, David	Served in the Revolution
Walker, James	Refugee
Walker, Joseph	Soldier, Ga. Cont. Line
Walker, Robert	Soldier, 3rd. Ga. Bn.
Walker, Sanders, Rev.	"Wilkes County. I do hereby certifi that the Revd. Sanders Walker was entered by Col. Dooly as Chaplain on pay before the surrender of Charles Town to the British. That he has lost considerable property by the British and Tories. Has twice left the State on account of the enemy. That after the first siege of Augusta he retreated with other Refugees over Broad River, till at my particular and ernest request he returned to use his influence with Maddox, Williams, and Waters, on behalf of the prisoners and distressed inhabitants. That he not only undertook the hazardous enterprize, but was of signal service to his country in prosecuting the instructions given him. I pledged myself to him that he should have every privilege of a Refugee,

and though as a Minister of the Gospel, he was exempted from bearing arms, I look on him as entitled to as much Bounty Land as any Refugee of his rank. Given under my hand this 2nd. Day of December, 1783. /S/ Elijah Clark, Col. The above relation of facts are within our knowledge. /S/ Daniel Coleman /S/ George Walton;" Sanders Walker was allowed the same quantity of land as a Major in Refugeeship

Walker, Thomas	Refugee
Walker, Thomas	Soldier, Ga. Cont. Line
Walker, William	Refugee Captain
Walker, William	Militia Soldier
Walker, William	Private in Bn. of Minute Men
Wall, Arthur	Soldier under command of Col. Elijah Clark until he was killed in service
Wall, David	Private in Bn. of Minute Men; went on Florida Expedition; resided in Ga. at time of enlistment
Wall, Francis	Private in Bn. of Minute Men
Wall, John	Private in Bn. of Minute Men
Wallace, William	Soldier, Ga. Cont. Line
Waller, Benjamin	Refugee
Waller, Jeremiah	Soldier in Bn. of Minute Men
Waller, John	Soldier, 3rd. Ga. Bn.
Wallis, Absalom	Refugee
Walsh, Edward	Acted as a Brigade Major; "I certify that Major Edward Walsh immediately after Savannah was taken by the British Troops, on my being sent to Augusta by General Lincoln, joined my command and acted as Brigade Major to the Militia and Troops that were then emboided to the time of my being made a prisoner after which I have been informed he joined General Wil-

liamson and was in service under him. Given under my hand Savannah, 15th. March, 1784. /S/ S. Elbert, Brigr. Genl." "I do hereby certify that after the Capture of genl. Elbert at Bryar Creek, Major Walsh joined the Command under Genl. Williamson & acted as an assistant to him until about the middle of June, 1779, at which time I left the General's family at Stono. /S/ Seth W. Cuthbert, 15th. March, 1784."

Walsh, Patrick	Major, Ga. Reg. Light Dragoons
Walthour, Andrew	Refugee
Walton, George	Refugee Captain
Walton, George	Militia Colonel of Chatham Co. Reg. of Militia

Walton, George Jr. — "This certifys that George Walton, the Younger, was appointed an Ensign in the First Georgia Continental Regiment the beginning of the year, 1776, was afterwards promoted to a Lieutenancy in the same Regiment and died in the service in the fall of 1777. Given under my hand at Savannah this 18th. March, 1784. /S/ Lackn. McIntosh, M. Genl."

Walton, Newell	Refugee
Walton, Robert	Refugee
Ward, Benjamin	Refugee
Ward, Hugh	Soldier in Bn. of Minute Men
Ward, John	Soldier in Bn. of Minute Men
Ward, Peter P.	Soldier in Bn. of Minute Men
Wardiman, Jacob	Soldier in Bn. of Minute Men
Wardman, Jacob	Soldier in Bn. of Minute Men
Ware, John	Refugee under command of Col. Elijah Clarke
Ware, Moses	Soldier, Ga. Cont. Line
Waring, Peter	Refugee
Warren, Elias	Refugee

Warren, Jeremiah	Refugee
Warren, John	Refugee
Waters, Rawley	Soldier in Bn. of Minute Men
Watson, Jacob	Soldier in Bn. of Minute Men
Watson, John	Soldier, 1st. Bn. of Minute Men
Watson, Levin	Refugee
Watson, Willis	Soldier in Bn. of Minute Men
Watts, Jacob	Private in Bn. of Minute Men
Waudin, John, Dr.	Surgeon, Ga. Line
Way, Edward	Refugee
Way, John	Soldier, Ga. Cont. Line
Way, John Jr.	Refugee
Way, John Sr.	Refugee
Way, Joseph	Soldier, Ga. Cont. Line
Way, William	Refugee
Way, William Jr.	Refugee
Webb, Jesse	Refugee
Webb, John	"These are to certify that John Webb belonged to the Second Company of Georgia Continental Artillery, from the first raising of said Company, until the reduction of Sunbury by the British Troops; when he was taken in Fort Morris, and with the rest of the Company sent aboard the prison ships where he remained several months a prisoner. Given under my hand this 3rd. day of March, 1784. /S/ John Dollar, Captain Lieutenand, said Company."
Webb, John	Refugee
Webb, John	Soldier
Webb, William	Refugee
Webb, William	Soldier
Webster, Abner	Private in Bn. of Minute Men
Webster, Benjamin	Private, 2nd. Cont. Reg., Ga. Line (Foot) under command of Lt. Francis Tennille and Lt. Col. J. Stirk; enlisted July 24,

	1777 and served for three years
Webster, Samuel	Private in Bn. of Minute Men
Webster, Thomas	Drummer, Ga. Cont. Line
Welborn, Curtis Jr.	Soldier in Bn. of Minute Men
Welborn, David	Militia Soldier under command of Captain Gunnels
Wells, Andrew	Refugee
Wells, Humphrey, Dr.	Refugee and Surgeon in Ga. State Legion under command of Col. James Jackson
Wells, Jacob	Soldier in Bn. of Minute Men
Wells, Jeremiah	Refugee
Wells, Joseph	Soldier in Bn. of Minute Men
Wells, Robert	Refugee
Welsh, Joshua	Sergeant in Bn. of Minute Men
Wereat, John	Refugee; was taken prisoner and carried to Charleston; was later exchanged
West, Samuel	Refugee Captain and Major
Westbrook, Stephen	Refugee Lt.
Whare, William	Refugee
Whatley, Samuel	Refugee
Whatley, Walton	Refugee under command of Col. Elijah Clark
Wheat, Hezekiah	Refugee
Whitaker, John	Captain of a Co. of Refugees
White, James	Refugee Captain under command of Col. Elijah Clarke until he was killed by the enemy
White, John	Refugee
White, Thomas	Soldier
Whiticil, John, Dr.	Refugee Surgeon in Reg. of Refugees under command of Col. Elijah Clarke; resided in South Carolina
Whitmore, Jonathan	Soldier, 3rd. Ga. Bn.; died while in service
Whitsets, John	Refugee under command of Col. Elijah Clarke
Whitt, Richard	Soldier, 1st. Bn. of Minute Men
Whitton, Osten	Soldier, 1st. Bn. of Minute Men

Wickman, John	Soldier in Bn. of Minute Men
Wideman, Adam	Refugee
Wiggins, William	Served "with Colonel Josiah Dunn's upon a scout, after torys, but was no lower down upon Ogeachee, Savannah side of the river, than Trippletts Ferry. ..."
Wilborn, Cooper	Soldier in Bn. of Minute Men
Wilford, Philip	Soldier in Bn. of Minute Men
Wilkins, David	Soldier in Bn. of Minute Men
Wilkins, Gabril	Soldier, 1st. Bn. of Minute Men
Wilkins, John	Soldier in Bn. of Minute Men
Wilkinson, John	Soldier in Bn. of Minute Men
Wilkinson, William	Soldier, 3rd. Reg., Ga. Cont. Line; was residing in Mecklinburg County, Virginia in January 1785
Williams, Butler	Soldier in Bn. of Minute Men
Williams, Carrol	Soldier, Ga. Cont. Line
Williams, Charles	Lt. in Bn. of Minute Men; deceased prior to May 1784; survived by Susanah Williams
Williams, Edward	Soldier in Bn. of Minute Men
Williams, Edward	Soldier in Bn. of Minute Men
Williams, Eli	Soldier in Reg. under command of Col. Leonard Marbury
Williams, George	Soldier in Bn. of Minute Men
Williams, George	Soldier, 1st. Bn. of Minute Men
Williams, John	Soldier, 3rd. Ga. Bn.
Williams, John	Soldier in Bn. of Minute Men
Williams, John	Soldier, 1st. Bn. of Minute Men
Williams, Joseph	Private in Bn. of Minute Men
Williams, Nathaniel	Soldier in 1st. Bn. of Minute Men
Williams, Samuel	Refugee
Williams, Samuel	Soldier in Bn. of Minute Men
Williams, Thomas	Soldier in Reg. under command of Col. Leonard Marbury
Williams, Thomas	Soldier in Bn. of Minute Men
Williamson, George	Refugee under command of Brig. Gen.

Williamson, Littleton	John Twiggs Soldier, 2nd. Ga. Reg., Cont. Line
Williamson, Micajah	Refugee Lt. Col.
Williamson, Robert	Refugee under command of Brig. Gen. John Twiggs
Williby, William	Private, 2nd. Ga. Cont. Reg.
Willie, Richard	Refugee; was deceased prior to May 1784
Willie, William	Refugee
Willis, Britain	Soldier, 1st. Bn. of Minute Men
Willis, Joseph	Soldier in Bn. of Minute Men
Wilson, David	Soldier in Bn. of Minute Men
Wilson, Hugh	Soldier in Bn. of Minute Men
Wilson, James	Refugee
Wilson, James	Soldier in Bn. of Minute Men
Wilson, John	Soldier in Bn. of Minute Men
Wilson, John	Refugee
Wilson, Robert	Soldier in Bn. of Minute Men
Wilson, Robert	Sergeant in Bn. of Minute Men
Wilson, Samuel	Soldier
Wilson, Samuel	Soldier in Bn. of Minute Men
Winfrey, Jacob	Captain; was deceased prior to December 1784
Winn, Joseph	Refugee
Winn, Peter	Refugee
Wise, James	Refugee
Wise, Peter	Soldier, Ga. Cont. Line
Wise, William	Refugee
Wisenor, John	Soldier, 1st. Bn. of Minute Men
Wolecon, Daniel	Refugee
Wolecon, Daniel Jr.	Refugee
Womack, Jesse	Soldier
Womack, John	Soldier, 2nd. Ga. Bn.
Wood, Edward	Captain; was deceased prior to May 1784
Wood, Henry	Refugee
Wood, James	Corporal, 3rd. Ga. Reg.
Wood, James	Lt. in Bn. of Minute Men
Wood, Joseph Sr.	"I certify that Mr. Joseph Wood, the eld-

	er, acted as Paymaster of the first Georgia Regiment of Continental Troops for the Summer of 1776 to October, 1777, when I left the State, as Deputy of his son, John Wood. Given under my hand Savannah, 1st. July, 1784. /S/ Lachn. McIntosh, M. Gen.;" Joseph Wood was at Purrysburg in 1779 and held the rank of Captain
Wood, Joshua	Refugee
Woodruff, Joseph	"Major of the different Artillery Companies in this state (and) was a Refugee from the same."
Woods, Hugh	Soldier in Bn. of Minute Men
Woods, John	Soldier in Bn. of Minute Men
Woods, Joshua	Soldier, 1st. Bn. of Minute Men
Woods, Joshua Jr.	Soldier in Bn. of Minute Men
Woods, Richard	Refugee
Wooten, Thomas	Refugee
Wooten, Thomas	Soldier in Bn. of Minute Men
Wright, Abednego	Refugee
Wright, Habbakkuk	Refugee under command of Col. William Candler
Wright, Meshack	Refugee under command of Col. William Candler
Wright, Shadrack	"This certifys that Shadrack Wright, esquire was appointed a Captain in the first Georgia Continental Regiment of Foot in February, 1776 and never resigned until he died which I am informed was the 26th August, 1781. Given under my hand at Savannah this 3rd. Febry., 1784. /S/ Lachn. McIntosh, Maj. Gen."
Wyche, Batt	Refugee
Wynn, Joshua	Refugee
Yarbery, William	Refugee
Yarbrough, James	Private in Bn. of Minute Men
Yesterday, Charles	Soldier in Reg. under command of Col.

	Leonard Marbury
York, James	Soldier in Bn. of Minute Men
York, James	Refugee
York, John	Refugee
Young, Anthony	Soldier in Bn. of Minute Men
Young, Daniel	Lt. in Bn. of Minute Men
Young, Edward	Refugee
Young, Edward	Private in Bn. of Minute Men
Young, Isham	Refugee
Young, Isham	Soldier in Bn. of Minute Men
Young, John	Soldier in Col. John Stuart's Bn. of Minute Men
Young, John Jr.	Private in Bn. of Minute Men
Young, John Jr.	Refugee
Young, John Sr.	Private in Bn. of Minute Men
Young, Peter	Refugee
Young, William	Refugee
Young, William	Soldier in Bn. of Minute Men
Young, William	Private in Bn. of Minute Men
Youngblood, Abraham	Soldier
Youngblood, Isaac	Soldier
Youngblood, James	Served in the Revolution
Youngblood, John	Militia Private
Youngblood, Peter	Refugee
Zettler, Daniel	Refugee; was deceased prior to January 1784
Zettler, Matthew	Refugee; was deceased prior to March 1784; survived by heir, Nathaniel Zettler
Zettler, Nathaniel	Refugee
Zinn, Jacob	Refugee; joined Col. William Candler's Reg. at 1st. siege of Augusta

LIST OF MEN WHO SERVED IN THE GEORGIA LINE IN THE OCONEE WAR, 1787 – 1790

ALL IN THE 1ST. REGIMENT, STATE TROOPS

Adare, Bozeman	Private Soldier
Anderson, Robert	Private, 8th. Co.
Andrekin, George	Soldier, 6th. Co.
Armstrong, Alexander	Soldier, 10th. Co.
Arnet, Edward	Soldier, 3rd. Co.
Ballard, John	Private, 1st. Co.
Bartlett, Nonrod	Soldier, 8th. Co.
Blandford, Richard	Private, 8th. Co.
Bragg, Benjamin	Lt. and Adjutant, 1st. Reg., State Troops
Breedlove, Benjamin	Soldier
Bruce, Daniel	Soldier, 6th. Co.
Bucklin, James	Private, 8th. Co.
Burke, Edward	Private, 1st. Co.
Burks, Edward	Soldier, 1st. Co.
Carter, Thomas	Soldier, 1st. Co.
Cheson, John	Private, 1st. Co.
Clack, James	Substitute, 1st. Co.
Clack, William	Substitute, 5th. Co.
Cochran, William	Soldier, 2nd. Co.
Colbert, Elisha	Private, 8th. Co.
Cooper, Phil	Soldier, 3rd. Co.
Cox, James	Substitute, 8th. Co.
Crouch, William	Soldier, 1st. Co.
Davis, James	Soldier, 9th. Co.
David, Thomas	Soldier
Dean, Thomas	Substitute, 3rd. Co.
Dobbs, Joseph	Lt., 8th. Co.
Easley, Roderick	Lt. and Quatermaster, 1st. Reg., State Troops
Edge, Joseph	Soldier, 7th. Co.; deceased prior to 1795
Edwards, James	Sergeant, 10th. Co.
Elliott, Thomas	Private, 5th. Co.
Farmer, William	Substitute, 2rd. Co.
Franklin, Thomas	Soldier, 6th. Co.
Furlow, John	Soldier, 3rd. Co.
Giles, John	Private, 8th. Co.
Glen, John	Private, 6th. Co.

Griffith, John	Private 1st. Co.
Hammock, Joseph	Soldier, 4th. Co.
Harris, Edward	Private, 1st. Co.
Harris, Michael	Soldier, 3rd. Co.
Harrison, Clem	Lt., 1st. Co.
Harrison, Jere	Private, 1st. Co.
Harvey, Robert	Sergeant, 6th. Co.
Hatherly, Hugh	Soldier, 8th. Co.
Holliday, William Sr.	Private, 5th. Co.
Hutson, Joseph	Soldier, 6th. Co.
Jackson, Jervis	Private, 4th. Co.
Johnson, George	Soldier, 1st. Co.
Johnson, James	Private, 9th. Co.
Jones, Edward	Lt., 1st. Co.
Landrum, John	Private, 9th. Co.
Lawler, John	Private, 10th. Co.
Lawrence, Miles	Soldier, 9th. Co.
Ledbetter, Henry	Soldier, 8th. Co.
Lockett, Thomas	Soldier, 3rd. Co.
Matthews, Isaac	Substitute, 10th. Co.
Matthews, John	Soldier, 9th. Co.
Matthews, Thomas	Soldier, 10th. Co.
McMullan, Alexander	Soldier, 6th. Co.
Mead, Minor	Sergeant, 7th. Co.
Meador, Joel	Sergeant Substitute, 7th. Co.
Meador, Jonas	Sergeant Substitute, 7th. Co.
Montcrief, Samuel	Soldier, 2nd. Co.
Moran, Michael	Sergeant, 6th. Co.
Moreman, Thomas	Sergeant, 5th. Co.
Mevlin, Matthias	Soldier, 1st. Co.
O'Barre, Robert	Soldier, 1st. Co.
Orr, John	Soldier, 5th. Co.
Owens, Thomas	Private, 1st. Co.
Pearce, William	Soldier; was deceased prior to Dec. 1809; was survived by brother, John Pearce
Pullen, Majors	Soldier, 8th. Co.
Reddy, James	Soldier, 10th. Co.

Reeves, Alexander	Lt., 4th. Co. (no first name given in original certificate; name furnished by Shelby Myrick and Gordon Smith, both of Savannah, Georgia)
Ross, John	Sergeant, 1st. Co.
Rumley, George	Soldier, 6th. Co.
Russell, George Jr.	Substitute, 1st. Co.
Ryan, Joseph	Major, 1st. Reg., State Troops
Sandell, John	Soldier, 6th. Co.
Short, Jonas	Substitute, 8th. Co.
Sims, Robert	Soldier, 1st. Co.
Smith, John	Soldier, 1st. Co.
Smith, Reubin	Substitute, 1st. Co.
Smith, Samuel	Private, 8th. Co.
Smith, William	Private, 2nd. Co.
Smith, William	Soldier, 1st. Co.
Stallings, James	Colonel
Stanbanks, John	Private, 5th. Co.
Stiff, William	Private, 6th. Co.
Stuman, John	Substitute, 8th. Co.
Sykes, Joshua	Soldier, 2nd. Co.
Terrill, Joseph	Private, 8th. Co.
Truball, John	Soldier, 6th. Co.
Tual, Thomas	Soldier, 6th. Co.
Tucker, Woodward	Soldier, 5th. Co.
Wilcox, Thomas	Soldier, 9th. Co.
Williamson, Charles	Captain of the 1st. Co.
Williford, James	Soldier, 6th. Co.
Wood, Etheldred	Lt., 2nd. Co.
Wood, James	"Washington, Feby 9th, 1790. I do certify that Capt. James Wood of the 1st. State Regiment was killed by the Indians the Twenty fifth day of March one thousand and seven hundred eighty eight and that his administrator is entitled to receive the Bounty and Pay. /S/ Thos Martin, I. Genl."

York, David   Soldier, 9th. Co.
Zimmerman, Simon   Private, 5th. Co.

APPENDIX

The complete appendix, with the exception of the photographs at the end, was compiled by Gordon Smith of Savannah, Georgia. Mr. Smith is presently (1983) president of the Sons of the Revolution in the State of Georgia. He probably is that state's leading authority on military history and it is with great pleasure that he has consented to have the following narrative included in this study.

THE GEORGIA CONTINENTAL ESTABLISHMENT

1775 − 1783

1. INFANTRY. Georgia had four battalions of foot brought into its Continental establishment between November of 1775 and the demise of the Continental Line in 1780. These four battalions, incorrectly called regiments upon occasion, comprised the units of the 1st. Georgia Regiment, authorized for Georgia by Congress on 16 September 1776. The 1st Regiment was actually an administrative or paper organization, especially with the creation of the three successive Georgia Brigades. These latter units were organized for field duty and were temporary in nature. Upon the re-establishment of the forces in Georgia in 1782, that state was authorized one battalion of troops, part foot and part light horse. The Georgia Continental battalions were as follows:

a. 1st GEORGIA BATTALION. Authorized by Congress on 4 November 1775. Officers appointed on 29-30 January 1776 by Georgia. Originally organized with eight companies, including a rifle company. Reorganized on 28 May 1778 into ten companies; grenadier and light infantry companies being added. The 1st Battalion was commanded as follows: Lachlan McIntosh from January 1776 to September 1776; Joseph Habersham from September 1776 to March 1778; and Robert Rae from March 1778 until his death in November of 1779. Lieutenant Colonel Francis Henry Harris became acting commander until the Georgia Continental Line disappeared in 1780.

b. 2d GEORGIA BATTALION. Authorized by Congress on 5 July 1776 as a musket battalion. Reorganized as ten companies on 28 May 1778. Commanded by Samuel Elbert from July 1776 until its final defeat and capture at Brier Creek in March 1779.

c. 3d GEORGIA BATTALION. Authorized by Congress on 5 July 1776 as a rifle battalion. Reorganized as ten companies on 28 May 1778. Commanded as follows: James Screven from July 1776 to

March 1778; John Stirk from March 1778 to October 1778. John McIntosh became acting commander until the remnants of the unit retired into South Carolina and disappeared.

d. 4th GEORGIA BATTALION. Authorized in the latter part of 1776. Officers were appointed by Georgia on 1 February 1777. Recruiting was done in Pennsylvania, Maryland, Virginia, and the Carolinas, having been initiated in August and September of 1777 with the recruiting of troops from several Connecticut Continental regiments at Peekskill, New York. The unit was largely made up of British deserters. The battalion marched south upon being raised and entered Savannah in January of 1778. Served as marines during the Florida Expedition of 1778. Its commander was Colonel John White, formerly of the 2d. North Carolina Regiment. He served from February 1777 to the Fall of 1779, when he was made a supernumerary colonel, his unit having been gradually destroyed.

e. 1st GEORGIA BATTALION. Organized 4 July 1782 at the impetus of General Nathanael Greene. Called variously the 1st Georgia Battalion, the Georgia Battalion, the 1st Georgia Regiment, or the Georgia Regiment. The unit was a foot battalion, but was to include two companies or troops of cavalry in the style of a legion. Ranks filled by Amercement Laws with former Georgia Tories. The men of the Georgia Battalion were furloughed according to prior Congressional resolution in July 1783 and subsequently discharged in December of that year (effective 3 November 1783) in accordance with Congressional resolution of 18 October 1783. Commanded by Major John Habersham

f. LIGHT INFANTRY. This independent corps was ordered created by General Robert Howe on 28 May 1778 and was composed of the four light infantry companies from the foot battalions. The light infantry was commanded by Lieutenant Colonel Francis Henry Harris of the 1st Georgia Battalion.

g. GRENADIERS. This independent corps was ordered created by

General Howe on 28 May 1778. Like the light infantry, it was composed of the four grenadier companies from the four foot battalions. The grenadiers were commanded by Major Francis Moore, of the 2d Georgia Battalion.

h. EXTRA OFFICERS CONTINGENT. Upon the re-establishment of the Georgia Battalion in 1782, supernumerary officers were enrolled as "Extra Officers". Such contingent consisted of about 25 officers. This corps had no combat mission, but seems to have been for pay and retention purposes only.

2. CAVALRY. Georgia had one regiment of light horse from 1776 to 1780. In 1782 Georgia was authorized one battalion of foot, which was to have two troops of cavalry. The Georgia Continental cavalry units were as follows.

a. GEORGIA LIGHT HORSE. Authorized as a full regiment by Congress on 24 July 1776. Was to be formed as a regiment of rangers, or mounted infantry, in the same manner as was the 3d South Carolina Regiment. Originally authorized ten companies or troops. Georgia had begun raising two independent troops of horse on state establishment in April of 1776. The First Troop, commanded by Captain William McIntosh, with Hatton Middleton as lieutenant, was stationed in the south on the Altamaha River. The Second Troop, commanded by Captain Leonard Marbury, with Thomas Hovenden as 1st lieutenant and Charles Middleton as 2d lieutenant, was stationed in the "back country" of the Ceded Lands. By July two additional troops of horse had been added to state establishment. The Third Troop was commanded by Captain Benjamin Few, with Ignatius Few as 1st lieutenant. The Fourth Troop was commanded by recently-promoted Captain Thomas Hovenden, with John Stewart as 1st lieutenant. These four companies were constituted as the "Georgia State Regiment of Horse", as authorized by the General Assembly of Georgia at its session of January 1776. When the news of the authorization of Congress for a regiment was received in Georgia, these four troops were placed on Continental establishment and six more troops were raised. On 5

November 1776 the Executive Council of Georgia augmented the regiment to twelve troops by accepting two additional units raised in the north (Lehancius DeKeyser and Samuel Scott). With a failure in recruiting, the regiment was reduced to four independent companies of 50 men each by Congress on 13 February 1778. The Georgia Light Horse was gradually destroyed in the actions of 1779. By the early part of that year, Colonel Marbury found his regiment in a state of collapse. He requested and received permission from General Benjamin Lincoln to raise an augmented, composite regiment containing South Carolina men as well as the remnants of his regiment then in existence. He and part of his command were captured in March 1779. Officers of the Georgia Light Horse were made supernumeraries on 1 January 1780. The Georgia Light Horse Regiment was originally called the 1st Georgia Regiment of Light Dragoons. With the ensuing confusion between the terms regiment and battalion (there then being three Georgia Continental foot battalions), the unit became known as the 4th Georgia Regiment of Light Horse. With the organization of the 4th Georgia Battalion of foot, the horse regiment became generally known as the Georgia Light Horse. Commanders of the regiment were as follows: William McIntosh from July 1776 to January 1777; John Baker from about February 1777 to August 1777; Leonard Marbury from October 1777 to the reduction of the regiment in 1780.

b. GEORGIA BATTALION (2 troops). At the authorization of the one Georgia battalion on 4 July 1782 such was to include two troops of cavalry. Due to a failure in recruiting, the troops were not raised.

3. ARTILLERY. Georgia was authorized three companies of artillery on Continental establishment. These companies were primarily for the fixed defense of Georgia's ports, but were to accompany the Georgia Brigade on the Florida Expeditions as required. Overall command of the Georgia Continental artillery was given to Major Charles Noel Romand DeLisle. Due to the failure in recruiting there were actually four companies of artillery prior to the fall of Savannah in 1778. After the

return of the patriots to Georgia in 1782, there were no new artillery units established for the state in its Continental organization. The artillery units were as follows:

a. 1st COMPANY OF ARTILLERY. Authorized by Congress on July 1776 for coast defense. Was to have 50 men. This "light artillery company" was stationed at Savannah and Tybee Island. It was commanded as follows: Alexander Phoenix from November 1776 to about December 1777 (died); George Young from about December 1777 to the fall of Savannah in December 1778. In November of 1778 Captain Young was granted three months leave. He apparently did not return to the unit, as Lieutenant William Johnson was later promoted to command the company. Johnson died in 1780 as a prisoner of war.

b. 2d COMPANY OF ARTILLERY. Authorized by Congress at the same time and on the same terms as the 1st Company. This unit was stationed at Sunbury (Fort Morris). It was commanded by Thomas Morris from 1776 to its surrender in January 1779.

c. 3d COMPANY OF ARTILLERY. Authorized by Georgia in July 1776 as a provincial company, but in anticipation of eventual Continental service. Authorized by Congress in February 1777. The unit was to be raised upon the completion of the first two companies. Was to consist of 53 officers and men. Raised initially on Salter's Island, now the site of Fort Jackson, in the Savannah River. It was soon moved to its battery Fort Bulloch at the Trustees Garden (this battery was to be expanded by the British as Fort Prevost and successfully defended by the Tory Captain Thomas Mills and his artillery company during the Storm of Savannah in October of 1779, subsequently being renamed Fort Wayne by the returning Georgia patriots). With the failure of recruiting and the deaths of its captain and lieutenant, the 3d Company of Artillery was merged with the 1st Company on 19 February 1778. The unit was commanded by Captain Thomas Lee from its inception until his death in February 1778. Lieutenant Laban Johnson became acting commander until the unit was merged with the 1st Company shortly thereafter.

d. 3d COMPANY OF ARTILLERY (reformed). Upon recommendation of General Robert Howe, Colonel Samuel Elbert, and Colonel John White, a new 3d Company of Artillery was organized on 3 April 1778. This unit was stationed at Savannah when the British captured the town. It was able to partly hold the rear of the doomed capital so as to allow the South Carolina Brigade and part of the Georgia Brigade to escape. It followed the remnants of the Georgia Brigade into South Carolina and attached itself to General Benjamin Lincoln's command. Ordered to join the Georgia Brigade at Augusta in January of 1779. The unit was back with Lincoln in April of that year at Black Creek. No later record. The unit was commanded by Captain Jean Pierre Andre Defaupeyret (called "Captain Defau" by the Americans).

4. NAVY. Like the Georgia Continental land forces, the Georgia Continental Navy had two lives. The first establishment lasted from July 1776 to its reduction in January of 1780. The second establishment lasted from July 1782 to the end of the war. In July 1776 the state of Georgia decided to build a fleet of six galleys for coastal defense. These vessels were to be row galleys, but were to carry lateen-rigged sails (two per galley). On 5 July 1776 the Congress had authorized the building of four such galleys for Georgia. When the state received this news, it turned to the establishment of its Continental Navy. Oliver Bowen was appointed Commodore of this branch in January 1777. The first two galleys were completed in September of 1776. These two vessels and the third to be completed were armed as follows: (a) one galley with an 18-pounder and swivels, (b) one galley with two 12-pounders and swivels, and (c) one galley armed with two 18-pounders, two 9-pounders, and four 6-pounders. In March of 1777 a galley made its first capture by taking a schooner in St. Marys River. In the Spring of 1777 the first three galleys, *Lee, Congress,* and *Washington,* took part in the Florida Expedition. On 19 April 1778 three of the galleys captured a schooner, sloop, and brig near Frederica. The Georgia Naval Board was established to handle the responsibilities of the Continental vessels. Commodore Bowen had a series of disputes with the

state authorities over command and control, however, and was suspended from command on 16 November 1778. Two of the galleys were beached and burned at the fall of Sunbury in January 1779. The last two galleys assisted in the evacuation up river of the Patriots at the fall of Savannah. They were captured in Savannah River after an unsuccessful attack on the British on 20 March 1779. There was also a Continental schooner in Georgia service in 1777. Although the Georgia Continental Navy ended in January of 1780, some of its officers and men continued to fight the British in privateers or armed galleys. Upon the re-establishment of the Georgia Patriot government in 1782, the Navy was formally reconstituted. On 29 July 1782 Georgia decided to purchase or build two galleys, to be mounted with eight guns each. The first was built by January of 1783 and the second was purchased on 12 February 1783. The Continental vessels in the Georgia Navy were as follows:

a. LEE. This galley was launched about September of 1776 and was fitted by December of that year. Armed with cannon and swivels. Carriage guns were fitted on skids so as to traverse at least four points each way on each bow. First commanded by Captain George Bunner, former master of the brig *Georgia Packet*, in which he had carried Georgia's three delegates to Philadelphia in July of 1775 to the Continental Congress. The lieutenant for the *Lee* was John Braddock (son of Captain David Cutler Braddock, a well-known naval commander in the French-Indian War), promoted to the command of the *Lee* by the time it was involved in the 1778 capture of the three British vessels off Frederica. Captain Jacob Milligan of South Carolina succeeded to command by March of 1779, when the galley was captured.

b. WASHINGTON. This galley was launched with the *Lee* and fitted in the same fashion. Its first commander was Captain Job Pray, who was eventually to enter state naval service before commanding the *Hinchinbrook* at the fall of Savannah. Robert Palmer was the lieutenant in the early part of 1777. Pray's subsequent lieutenant was John Newdigate, who succeeded him in command. The galley was commanded by Captain John Hardy (Hardee) when it participated in the capture of the three British vessels in 1778. Commanded by 1779 by Captain Gilbert Harrison, a former privateer captain, the galley was beached and burned on Ossabaw Island in January of 1779 at the fall of Sunbury.

c. CONGRESS. This galley was launched and fitted by March 1777. It was first commanded by Captain Joseph Woodruff, who had formerly commanded the provincial marines. He was succeeded in command by Captain John Hardy. Hardy was captured at the fall of Sunbury and was succeeded by Captain Robert Campbell, commander at the taking of the galley in March of 1779. Sheraud De Longig was commissioned as lieutenant of the *Congress* in April of 1778.

d. BULLOCH. This galley was launched about June of 1777. Its first commander was Captain Archibald Hatcher, who died in August of 1778. He and his galley participated in the capture of the three British vessels off Frederica in April of that year. He was succeeded in command by Captain Thomas Maxwell. Captain Maxwell was succeeded in turn by Captain John Bacon by 1779, when the galley was beached and destroyed on Ossabaw Island with the *Washington*. William Lambeth was a lieutenant of one of the Continental galleys, possibly the *Bulloch*. He died about October of 1778.

e. GEORGIA PACKET. In November of 1776 Lieutenant Isaac Buck was promoted to command this schooner and ordered to Savannah. He arrived at that port in April of 1777. This vessel was apparently captured at a subsequent date. By 1780 Buck was serving on a privateer out of Philadelphia, in which type of service he continued for the duration of the war.

f. STATE GALLEY. By January of 1783 Captain John Brown, former commander of the Savannah scout boat, commanded a galley in Georgia service. The *State Galley* was one of those commissioned under the authority of Congress. The keel of this galley was laid in August of 1782, and the vessel was finished about October of that year. It was built by John Morel at Beaulieu in Chatham County. It carried four 9-pound cannonades, some swivels, and two prow guns. A second galley was to be built, but there is no evidence that it was ever completed.

g. SAILORS DELIGHT (or simply, Delight). This galley was purchased by Continental authority from Captain John Howell. Before the Revolution, the Welsh-born Howell had been a watchmaker of St. Paul's Parish. At the outbreak of the war he was commissioner captain of the 1st Company of foot militia in the Second Regiment, taking his unit on an expedition into the "Back Country" to suppress Tories in January of 1776. He also supplied much of the iron utilized in constructing the first four galleys in Georgia Continental service. At the surrender of Sunbury he was captured, but violated his parole to take command of a Continental sloop sailing out of the Carolinas. Subsequently he became captain of a privateer galley which raided the Georgia coast. This vessel was described as rowing with 26 oars, armed with 5 swivels, with an on board crew of only 14 men—a small galley. Howell sold this galley to Georgia at Continental reimbursement on 12 February 1783. This galley was subsequently ordered sold at public auction in September of 1783. On 27 August 1790 Howell was commissioned captain of the Augusta Volunteer Artillery Company. This company, under Howell's command, fired the welcome salutes to President Washington upon the latter's visit to Georgia the following year. In 1791 Howell became the commander of the U.S. Revenue Cutter *Eagle,* and later the Cutter *Jefferson.* Howell died in 1814 at St. Marys, Georgia.

OFFICERS OF THE GEORGIA CONTINENTAL LINE, NAVY, AND MILITARY AND CIVIL STAFFS

GENERAL. This list does not include assistant commissaries for the civil staff in Georgia, regimental commissaries, commanders of the Southern Department nor all of the military staff of the Southern Department. It also does not include such men as the Continental Indian Commissioners, Auditors General, recruiting agents, and acting Continental commanders for Georgia (Parker, et al.). Three of the officers listed below were not really Continentals; one (Hughes) being killed before his unit was put on Continental Establishment, one (Pugh) being dismissed before his unit was put on the establishment, and one (Rees) being captured before Congress could act on his appointment. These men are included, however, since State and Continental authorities ruled that they be treated as having served with such commissions. Names are shown as most commonly spelled where no original signatures could be found. Grades shown are highest verified Continental grade in active service. By order of Congress on 8 January 1780, no more line officers were to be retained in Georgia service than were necessary for two regiments. All left out in the new arrangement were made supernumeraries. At the same time all officers of the galley service (Navy) and light horse were made supernumeraries.

1. AITKEN, James, Chaplain, 4th Bn., former chaplain of 4th N.C. Regt.
2. ALEXANDER, Adam, Sur. Mate, Hospital, captured 1778, (brother of James), (died 3 March 1812)
3. ALEXANDER, James, Cpt.-Lt., 1st Co., Arty, traitor (died 11 September 1805)
4. ALLEN, Moses, Chaplain, Gen. Staff, captured, drowned 1779
5. ALLISON, Henry, Lt., 2d Bn., retired 1782 (killed in duel July 1789)
6. ANDERSON, ------, Lt., Lt. Horse, dead by October 1777
7. ARTHUR, Francis, 2d Lt., 1st Bn.
8. ASBEY, William, 2d Lt., Lt. Horse, also "Aspey"
9. BACON, John, Capt., Navy
10. BAKER, John, Col., Lt. Horse, resigned 1777 (died 1 June 1792)

11. BAKER, William, Maj., Lt. Horse
12. BARD, John, Capt., 2d Bn., captured 1778, returned to New York 1779 while prisoner, resigned.
13. BAUGH, Alexander C., 1st Lt., 2d Bn., resigned 1778
14. BAYLY, James, Lt., 2d Bn.
15. BAYLY, Joseph, Lt., 2d Bn., same as James?
16. BEAMS, ‑‑‑‑‑, Lt., Lt. Horse, from S.C., returned to S.C. sick 1777
17. BENNIS, John, Capt., 4th Bn., died in service
18. BERRIEN, John, Capt., 1st Bn., wounded 1777, also Bde MAJ, Gen. McIntosh, (died 5/6 November 1815)
19. BEVILL, George, Ens., 3d Bn.
20. BILBO, John, Lt., Lt. Horse, discharged 1778 (mortally wounded and captured; died 8 May 1780)
21. BLOUNT, Jacob, Sur. Mate, Navy, kidnapped 1778 (dead by 27 January 1784)
22. BOOKER, Gideon, Capt., 3d Bn., captured 1779, made supernumerary 1782
23. BOSTICK, Chesley, Capt., 1st Bn., captured 1778 (died 2 January 1808)
24. BOWEN, Oliver, Commodore, Navy suspended 1778, from R.I. (died 11 July 1800)
25. BOX, Philip, Cmy. Hosp., Civ. Staff (died 16 December 1781)
26. BRADDOCK, John, Capt., Navy (died 16 June 1797)
27. BRADLEY, James, Capt., Lt. Horse
28. BROSSARD, Celerine, Capt., 4th Bn., leave to France 1782
29. BROWN, ‑‑‑‑‑, Ens.
30. BROWN, ‑‑‑‑‑, Maj., 4th Bn., adjutant
31. BROWN, James, Lt., 4th Bn., captured 1779
32. BROWN, John, Capt., Navy (died October 1785)
33. BROWN, Thomas, 1st Lt., 2d Bn., killed at Stono Ferry, 20 June 1779
34. BROWNSON, Nathan, Surgeon, So. Dept. (died October 1796)
35. BRYAN, James, Capt., Lt. Horse, also "Bryant"
36. BRYAN, James, Lt., 4th Bn., captured 1779 (died 1832)
37. BRYDIE, David, Surgeon, 2d Bn., captured 1778, died as prisoner
38. BRYSON, Nicholas, Lt., Lt. Horse, also "Broxton", "Braston"

39. BUCK, Isaac, Capt., Navy, Continental schooner
40. BUDD, Charles, Capt., resigned
41. BUDD, Thomas, Capt., 4th Bn., resigned 1778
42. BUGG, Jeremiah, Capt., Lt. Horse, resigned 1777 (died about 1787, Richmond County, Georgia)
43. BUGG, William, 1st. Lt., Lt. Horse, captured 1780
44. BUNNER, George, Capt., Navy, captured 1776
45. BURK(E), John, Lt., Lt. Horse
46. CADE, Drury, Capt., Lt. Horse, retired (died 20 August 1838)
47. CALDWELL, John, Lt., Lt. Horse, captured
48. CALENDER, Ebenezer, Sur. Mate, 3d Bn., captured 1779
49. CAMPBELL, John, Ens., 4th Bn.
50. CAMPBELL, John, 2d Lt., 1st Co., Arty, captured 1778
51. CANNON, Henry, Lt., Lt. Horse
52. CARNEY, Arthur, Capt., 1st Bn., captured 1777, traitor (died during war)
53. CARSWELL, John, 1st Lt., 4th Bn., captured 1779 (died March 1817)
54. CATER, John, Surgeon, Lt. Horse, from S.C. (died in 1782)
55. CHISOLM, Thomas, Lt. Col., 4th Bn. (died 21 October 1789)
56. CLARK, Charles, Lt., 3d Bn., same as John C. Clark?
57. CLARK, John C., Lt., 3d Bn.
58. CLARK, John J., Capt., 2d Bn., also "Clarke"
59. CLAY, Joseph, Lt. Col., Civ. Staff, Ga. and So. Dept. (died 15 December 1804)
60. CODDINGTON, Francis, Cmy. Issues, Civ. Staff, captured 1779 (died 24 November 1792)
61. COLE, Josiah, Lt., 3d Bn.
62. COLLINS, Cornelius, 1st Lt., 2d Bn., captured 1779 (died December 1791)
63. COLOMB, Pierre de la, Capt., Lt. Horse, captured 1778 (General in France)
64. COLSON, Jacob, Capt., 1st Bn., resigned, (died 1778)
65. CONNOLY, -----, Capt., 1st Bn.
66. CONNOR, Daniel, Lt., not documented
67. CONNOR, John, Lt., Lt. Horse
68. COOK, Joseph, Lt., Lt. Horse

69. COOK, Isham, Capt., 2d Bn., died in service, also "Shem" Cook
70. COOK, Ranes, Capt., 3d Bn., captured 1779
71. COOPER, John, Capt., Lt. Horse, Lt. Col. in militia
72. COWEN, Edward, Capt., 4th Bn., captured 1779, (died 29 January 1800), also "Cowan"
73. CRAMDEN, Ralph Edward, Sur. Mate, 2d Bn., captured 1779
74. CUNNINGHAM, John, Capt., 2d Bn., captured 1778, Lt. Col. in militia (died 12 March 1829)
75. CUTHBERT, Alexander Daniel, Capt., 1st & 3d Bn., captured 1779 and 1782
76. CUTHBERT, Seth John, Maj., 2d Bn., (died 10 November 1788)
77. DAVENPORT, Thomas, Surgeon, 3d Bn., captured 1778, died in 1780
78. DAVENPORT, Thomas, Lt., 2d Bn., captured 1778, Grenadier Company
79. DAY, Joseph M., Bvt. Maj., 4th Bn., captured 1778, (died January 1793)
80. DE BRODIE, ------, Lt., 4th Bn.
81. DEFAUPEYRET, Jean Pierre Andre, Capt., 3d Co., Arty, also "Defau"
82. DEJONG, Jacob, Surgeon, Navy
83. DE KEYSER, Lehancius, Maj., Lt. Horse (moved to Fayetteville, N.C. after war)
84. DE LA PLAIGNE, Emanuel Pierre, Capt., 1st Bn., to France 1777 (died 1788)
85. DELAPLAINE, Joseph, Surgeon, 4th Bn., resigned 1779
86. DELISLE, Charles Noel Romand, Maj., Artillery, to San Domingo 1777
87. DE LONGIG, Sheraud, 2d Lt., Navy
88. DEMERE, Raymond, Maj., Civ. Staff, Deputy Commissary General (died 22 May 1791)
89. DEPATHIER, ------, Lt., 4th Bn.
90. DESPILIERS, ------, Lt., 4th. Bn.
91. DE VALIELL, Jean Dufort Chevalier, 2d Lt., 3d Co., Arty
92. DEVEAUX, Peter, Maj., Mil. Staff, A.D.C. (died 6 October 1826)
93. DICKINSON, Elijah, Lt., Lt. Horse (also "Dickenson" and Dickerson")

94. DICKSON, Walter, Lt., 4th Bn., captured 1779, also "Dixon"
95. DOHERTY, -----, Lt., Lt. Horse, also "Dogherty"
96. DOLLAR, John, Cpt.-Lt., 2d Co., Arty, captured 1779 (died 9 October 1797)
97. DONALDSON, -----, Capt., Lt. Horse
98. DOOLY, George, 2d Lt., 3d Bn., Major in militia
99. DOOLY, John, Capt., Lt. Horse, Colonel in militia, surrendered 1780, murdered 1780
100. DOOLY, Thomas, Capt., 2d & 3d Bn., also Major in militia, killed 22 July 1777
101. DOTY, Hull, Lt., Navy, also "Dooly". Doty of Liberty County (d.ca 1793)
102. DOUGLASS, David, ADC to Elbert, captured 1779
103. DOWNMAN, Raleigh, Capt., 3d Bn., also Lt. Horse
104. DUCOIN(S), (DECOSTIA), John Francis Borigan, Capt., 1st Bn. captured 1780
105. DUMOUCHETT, John, Lt., 3d Bn.
106. DUVAL, Daniel, Capt., 2d Bn. (?) killed
107. EDWARDS, John, Lt., Navy
108. ELBERT, Samuel, Brig. Gen., 2d Bn., captured 1779 (died 1 November 1788)
109. EMAN, John, 2d Lt., 1st Bn.
110. ETES, Thomas D., Lt., 3d Bn.
111. EUSTACE, John Skey, Maj, 4th Bn; resigned 1780; moved to Fayetteville, N.C. after the war; also Col, Adj. Gen.; promoted to Gen. (died August 1805)
112. FARISH, Robert, Lt., Lt. Horse
113. FAULKNER, Joseph, Capt., Lt. Horse, also "Faulkes", "Fowlkes", etc.
114. FEW, Benjamin, Capt., Lt. Horse, Colonel in militia
115. FEW, Ignatius, Capt., Lt. Horse, captured 1777, resigned, (died 18 February 1819)
116. FITZPATRICK, Patrick, Capt., 4th Bn., killed
117. FRASER, -----, Lt., Lt. Horse, killed in action 1777
118. FRASER, John, Capt., 3d Bn., captured 1778, returned to Virginia about 1779, also "Frasier"
119. GASTON, Alexander M., Lt., from S.C.

120. GATES, Andrew, Capt., 3d Bn., from Virginia
121. GERRARD, John, Capt., 3d Bn. & Lt. Horse, killed in ambush August 1777
122. GILMORE, William, Lt., Lt. Horse, also "Gilman", "Gilmour"
123. GIRARDEAU, John Bohun, D.C.G.I., Civ. Staff, resigned 1777 (died 1784)
124. GLASCOCK, Thomas, 1st Lt., 1st Bn. (died 9 March 1810)
125. GOFFE, Daniel, Ens., 2d Bn.
126. GOODIN, ─────, Lt., Lt. Horse, also "Gooden"
127. GREEN, John, Capt., 1st Bn., resigned (died 7 January 1799)
128. HABERSHAM, John, Maj., 1st Bn., captured 1778 and 1779 (died 19 November 1799)
129. HABERSHAM, Joseph, Lt. Col., 1st Bn., resigned 1778 (died 18 November 1815)
130. HANCOCK, George, Capt., 2d Bn., discharged 1779
131. HANDLEY, George, Maj., 1st Bn., captured 1780 (died 17 September 1793)
132. HARDY, John, Capt., Navy, captured (died 19 February 1790), also "Hardee"
133. HARRIS, Francis Henry, Lt. Col., 1st Bn., died 1781 in commission
134. HARRISON, Gilbert, Capt., Navy
135. HARVIE, ─────, Capt., traitor, cashiered
136. HARVEY, Alexander, Surgeon, Sunbury detachment
137. HATCHER, Archibald, Capt., Navy, died 1778, also "Hatchet"
138. HATCHET, Robert, Lt., Navy
139. HATTON, Josiah, Lt., 3d Bn.
140. HAWLING, Solomon, Surgeon, captured 1779
141. HAYES, Arthur, 1st Lt., 4th Bn., captured 1779 (died January 1790)
142. HENDLY, Philo, 1st Lt., 2d Co., Arty, captured 1779, also "Henly"
143. HERD, John, Capt., Engineer, died 14 February 1778, also "Hurd", not same as John Heard of Wilkes County
144. HICKS, Isaac, Capt., 3d Bn., captured 1779, returned to Virginia in 1779
145. HILL, James, 2d Lt., 2d Bn.

146. HILL, John, Lt., Lt. Horse, unconfirmed by original sources
147. HILL, William, Capt., Lt. Horse
148. HILLARY, Christopher, 1st Lt., 4th Bn., captured 1779 (died 18 February 1796)
149. HOLMES, John, Chaplain, 1st Bn., captured (died 30 March 1784)
150. HORNBY, William, Capt., 4th Bn., captured 1778, killed 1779
151. HOUSTOUN, James, Surgeon, 1st Bn., 1778 captured.
152. HOVENDEN, Thomas, Lt. Col., 4th Bn., died 16 April 1778
153. HOWE, Robert, Capt., 2d Bn., died in commission
154. HOWELL, Caleb, Capt., 1st Bn., Colonel in militia
155. HOWELL, John, Capt., Navy, captured 1779, also Captain in militia (died 1814)
156. HUGHES, Nathaniel, Lt., 3d Co., Arty, killed September 1776 (before Continental)
157. JACKSON, Samuel, Lt., unconfirmed by original sources (died 2 May 1836)
158. JARRATT, Devereaux, Capt. (died 17 April 1816)
159. JENKINS, John, 2d Lt., 1st Bn.
160. JETER, Andrew, Capt., 3d Bn.
161. JETER, Thomas, Lt., 3d Bn., cashiered 1778
162. JOHNSON, Laban, Capt.-Lt., 3d Co., Arty
163. JOHNSON, Seybourne, 2d Lt., 1st Co., Arty
164. JOHNSON, William, Capt., 1st Co., Arty, died as prisoner 1780
165. JONES, Abraham P., Bvt. Lt., 2d Bn. (died 28 January 1831)
166. JONES, John Jr., Maj., Mil. Staff, killed 9 October 1779
167. JORDAN, William, 1st Lt., 4th & 1st Bn. (died 16 January 1792)
168. KELL, John, D.C.I., Civ. Staff (died 27 November 1784)
169. LAMBETH, William, Lt., Navy, died 1778
170. LANE, Joseph, Maj., 3d Bn., captured 1779, made supernumerary in 1780 (died in 1801)
171. LANE, William, Capt., 2d Bn., also "Lain"
172. LEE, Thomas, Capt., 3d Co., Arty, died February 1778
173. LEWIS, Evan, Sur. Mate, So. Hosp., died in service, held rank of Capt.
174. LLOYD, Benjamin, Lt., 2d Bn., later of the South Carolina Continental Artillery
175. LOVE, John, Sur. Mate, 1st Bn. (died 25 April 1809)

176. LOVE, William, Adjutant, 3d Bn., resigned 1778, also "Lowe"
177. LOWE, —————, Capt., same as Philip?
178. LOWE, Philip, Maj., 4th Bn., captured, retired 1780 (died 1785)
179. LOWE, William, Lt., 1st Bn., captured 1779
180. LUCAS, John, Bvt. Maj., 1st Bn, 3d Bn, and 4th Bn, captured 1778
181. McCANTY, John, 1st Lt., 3d Bn.
182. McCUMBER, Matthew, Lt., Navy, captured
183. McDANIEL, Williams, Lt., Lt. Horse
184. McDONALD, William, Lt., Lt. Horse, also 4th Bn.
185. McFARLAND, James, Capt., Lt. Horse, retired
186. McGOWEN, —————, Lt., killed 18 May 1777
187. McINTOSH, John, Lt. Col., 3d Bn., captured 1779 (died 12 November 1826)
188. McINTOSH, Lachlan, Brig. Gen., Georgia Brigade, captured 1780 (died 20 February 1806)
189. McINTOSH, Lachlan, Capt., 1st Bn., son of William (died 21 December 1805)
190. McINTOSH, Lachlan, Lt., 4th Bn., also QM for Lt. Horse, son of Lachlan (died 15 February 1783)
191. McINTOSH, William, Lt. Col., Lt. Horse, resigned 1777 (died 7 February 1801)
192. McINTOSH, William, Capt., 1st Bn., captured 1778, son of Lachlan (died 1 December 1799)
193. McKINNE, Matthew, Surgeon, 4th Bn., captured
194. McKINNEY, James, Lt., 4th Bn., formerly 5th N.C. Regt., also "McKinne", "McKanna"
195. McKINNEY, John, Lt., 3d Bn., dismissed 1778
196. McLEUR, John, Capt., Navy, also "McCleur", etc., not same as Captain and Major of the 1st Regt., Georgia Militia
197. MARBURY, Horatio, Cornet, Lt. Horse
198. MARBURY, Leonard, Lt. Col., Lt. Horse, captured March 1779 (died 22 September 1796)
199. MARTIN, John, Capt., 1st Bn. (died 27 January 1786)
200. MATTHEWS, William, Capt., Deputy Muster Master General Georgia captured 1778
201. MAXWELL, Josiah, 1st Lt., 3d Bn., captured 1779, also given as

"Joseph" Maxwell
202. MAXWELL, Thomas, Capt., Navy (died 15 March 1795)
203. MEANLEY, John, 1st Lt., 3d Bn., captured 1779 (died 24 December 1788)
204. MELVIN, George, Capt., 4th Bn., captured 1780, made supernumerary 1782 (died December 1788)
205. MIDDLETON, Charles Starky, Capt., Lt. Horse, resigned 1777
206. MILLER, Elisha, Capt., 2d Bn. (died 1800)
207. MILTON, John, Maj., 1st Bn., captured 1777, retired 1782 (died 19 October 1817)
208. MITCHELL, John, 1st Lt., 1st Bn. and 3d Bn., captured 1778 resigned October 1782
209. MITCHELL, Josiah, Lt.
210. MITCHELL, Thomas, 1st Lt., 3d Bn.
211. MOORE, Francis, Maj., 2d Bn., captured 1778, killed 7 April 1782
212. MOREL, John, Capt., captured, Lt. Horse (died 1802)
213. MORRIS, Thomas, Capt., 2d Co., Arty, captured 1779, died 1781
214. MORRISON, John, 1st Lt., 2d Bn., retired 1782 (died 5 January 1802)
215. MOSBY, John, Capt., 2d Bn., captured 1779
216. MOSBY, Littleberry, Capt., 2d Bn., captured 1778, Colonel in Va. Militia 1780-1782 (died January 1809)
217. MOSBY, Robert, Lt., 2d Bn., captured 1778, returned to Virginia in 1780
218. NASH, Clement, Capt., 3d Bn., captured twice, died 1777
219. NETHERLAND, Benjamin, Lt., 2d Bn.
220. NETHERLAND, Thomas, Lt.
221. NEWDIGATE, John, Capt., Navy, died 1783
222. NEWMAN, Daniel, Surgeon, Hosp. Dept.
223. NORTHINGTON, Jabez, 2d Lt., 3d Bn., also "Norrington"
224. NORWAY, Anthony, Adjutant, Lt. Horse
225. ODINGSELLS, Benjamin, 1st Lt., 1st Bn., died in service in October of 1781
226. PALMER, Robert, Lt., Navy
227. PANNILL, Joseph, Lt. Col., 4th Bn., retired 1782
228. PARISH, Robert, Lt., 2d Bn.
229. PATTY, Bernard, Lt., 4th Bn., also "Petty"

230. PAYNE, Thomas, Bvt. Capt., 2d Bn., also "Paine", captured 1778
231. PEARRE, Nathaniel, Capt., 3d Bn., also "Perry"
232. PENDLETON, Nathaniel, Maj., A.D.C., General Nathanael Greene (died 20 October 1821)
233. PHILLIPS, John, Capt., 3d Bn.
234. PHOENIX, Alexander, Capt., 1st Co., Arty, died 1777
235. PIERCE, William Jr., Bvt. Maj., A.D.C. So. Dept. (died 10 December 1789)
236. POPE, John, Lt. Horse, resigned 1777
237. PORTER, Benjamin, Maj., 2d Bn.
238. PORTER, Robert, Lt.
239. PORTER, Thomas, Lt., 2d Bn.
240. POWELL, James, Lt., 4th Bn., resigned 1778
241. PRAY, Job, Capt., Navy (died 29 April 1789)
242. PUGH, James, Lt., Lt. Horse, decommissioned 1776 (not Continental)
243. RAE, James, Deputy Commissary General of Purchases, Civ. Staff, also Cmr. Ind. Affairs (died March 1789)
244. RAE, John, Lt., 1st & 2d Bn.
245. RAE, Robert, Col., 1st Bn., died November 1779
246. READ, William, Surgeon, So. Hosp., So. Dept.
247. REES, David, J.A., Gen. Staff, temporary commission, captured 1779 (died 29 March 1832 near Norristown, Pa.)
248. RICE, Nathaniel, Maj., Civ. Staff, D.P.M.G., Georgia
249. RIDGELY, Frederick, Sur. Mate, 2d Bn.
250. ROACH, William, Lt.
251. ROBERTS, Daniel, Lt. Col., 2d Bn., captured, died 18 November 1779
252. ROBINSON, -----, Lt., Lt. Horse, wounded in action 4 May 1777, resigned 26 November 1777, also "Robeson", "Robertson"
253. ROCHE, Matthew, Lt., 2d Bn., captured, adjutant
254. ROLFES, Frederick, D.C.P., Civ. Staff, from East Florida (died 1783)
255. ROLFES, George, C.P., Civ. Staff
256. RUTLEDGE, William, Lt., 4th Bn.
257. ST. PIERS, -----, Capt., Engineer, "St. Pierre"?
258. SALTER, John, Capt., Lt. Horse

259. SARZEDAS, David, Lt., resigned, (moved to South Carolina after the war)
260. SCOTT, Alexander, Chaplain, 1st Bn.
261. SCOTT, Samuel, Maj., Lt. Horse, wounded March 1778, retired 18 Jan. 1779 (died 20 June 1822)
262. SCOTT, Thomas, Capt., 3d and 2d Bn., resigned 1778
263. SCOTT, William, Capt., 3d Bn., captured 1779
264. SCREVEN, James, Lt. Col., 3d Bn., resigned 1778, brigadier general in militia (mortally wounded in battle 22 November 1778, died 24 November 1778)
265. SCRIMSGER, Charles, Lt., 1st Bn. (died 29 September 1804)
266. SEIXAS, Abraham Mendes, Lt., 1st Bn., resigned, (died 9 April 1799)
267. SHARPE, James Boyd, Surgeon
268. SHEFTALL, Mordecai, D.C.I. Civ. Staff, captured 1778 (died 6 July 1797)
269. SHICK, Frederick, 1st Lt., 2d Bn., captured 1781
270. SIMPSON, Robert, Lt., 4th Bn.
271. SMITH, Andrew, Sur. Mate, 2d Bn.
272. SMITH, Burrell, Capt., 3d Bn., resigned 1778, Major in militia (killed 8 August 1779)
273. SMITH, Randolph, Lt., 3d & 2d Bn.
274. SMITH, William, Capt., 2d Bn.
275. STEDMAN, James, Capt., 4th Bn., killed 1780
276. STEWART, John, Capt., Lt. Horse
277. STIRK, John, Col., 3d Bn., resigned 1778
278. STIRK, Samuel, J.A., Gen. Staff, captured (died 14 July 1793)
279. STRONG, John, D.C.I., Civ. Staff
280. STROTHER, William D., Lt., 2d Bn., resigned 1778 (killed as volunteer 22 November 1778)
281. SUTCLIFFE, John, A.D.Q.M., Civ. Staff, Captain
282. SUTTON, ------, Lt., 4th Bn.?
283. SUTTON, Thomas, Lt., 3d Co., Arty, resigned 1778
284. TAARLING, Peter, Col, Civ. Staff, Q.M.G., resigned 1778
285. TAYLOR, James, Capt., 1st Bn.
286. TAYLOR, Thomas, Capt. 4th Bn., adjutant, colonel in militia
287. TEMPLETON, Andrew, Capt., 4th Bn., captured 1779, killed 12

May 1780
288. TENNILL, Francis, Capt., 2d Bn.
289. TETARD, Benjamin, Sur. Mate, 4th Bn. (died 31 March 1800)
290. THREADGILL, Thomas, Capt., 3d Bn. (moved to N.C. after war)
291. TREVOR, John, Lt., Navy
292. TURNER, David, Capt.-Lt., 1st Co., Arty, died 1778
293. TURNER, William, Lt., 2d Bn.
294. WADE, Nehemiah, Q.M., Civ. Staff (died 1791)
295. WAGNON, John Peter, 1st Lt., 3d Bn., captured 1779 (moved to Tennessee after war)
296. WALKER, Benjamin, Capt., Lt. Horse
297. WALL, William, Capt., 3d Bn.
298. WALSH, Edward, Bde-Maj., Ga. Bde
299. WALSH, Patrick, Capt., Lt. Horse, Adjutant
300. WALTER, John, Lt., 3d Bn.
301. WALTON, George, D.C.P., Civ. Staff, Colonel in militia, signer of Declaration of Independence (died 2 February 1804)
302. WALTON, George, Capt., 1st Bn., died 15 September 1777
303. WALTON, George, Lt., Lt. Horse, same as above?
304. WALTON, Jesse, Capt., 1st Bn., killed
305. WALTON, John, Lt.
306. WALTON, Nathaniel, Lt.
307. WALTON, Robert, Capt., 2d Bn., also 1st Bn.(?)
308. WARD, Robert, Lt., 2d Bn., killed 18 May 1777
309. WASHINGTON, Thomas, Lt., 4th Bn., Major of Georgia State Legion (executed 23 March 1791) real name "Walsh"
310. WAUDIN, John Baptist, Surgeon, 3d Co., Arty & Ga. Line, captured 1780 (died October 1787), organized the Pocotaligo Hunters in December of 1775
311. WAUDIN, John William, Lt., 2d Bn., pay master
312. WEREAT, John, Agent for Marine Committee of Continental Congress, Civ. Staff, captured (died 25 January 1799)
313. WEST, Samuel, Capt., Lt. Horse (died 18 March 1795)
314. WHITE, James, Capt., 3d Bn.
315. WHITE, John, Col., 4th Bn., wounded and captured in 1779, died 1780, formerly of 2d N.C. Regt.
316. WILLIAMS, William, Capt., Lt. Horse

317. WILSON, John, Capt., 2d Bn.
318. WINFREE, Jacob, Capt., 2d Bn., died 1778, from Va.
319. WINFREE, Jesse, Capt., 2d Bn., also "Winfield"
320. WOOD, Edward, Capt., 2d Bn., captured 1779, resigned before 1780
321. WOOD, Henry, Surgeon, 3d Bn.
322. WOOD, John, Paymaster, 1st Bn., pay rank of Captain
323. WOODRUFF, Joseph, Capt., Navy, acting Adjutant and Pay master of 4th Bn., also Major and Colonel in state service (died January 1799)
324. WRIGHT, John, Capt., 2d Bn.
325. WRIGHT, John G., Surgeon
326. WRIGHT, Shadrack, Capt., 1st & 4th Bn., captured 1778, died in service
327. WYLLY, ------, Lt., 3d Bn., same as Thomas?
328. WYLLY, Richard, D.Q.M.G., Civ. Staff, captured (died 11 October 1801)
329. WYLLY, Thomas, Capt., 2d Bn., (died 31 May 1846 in 84th year of age)
330. YOUNG, George, Capt., 1st Co., Arty., also "Yonge", "Younge", died in service

OFFICERS OF THE AMERICAN CONTINENTAL AND FRENCH REGULAR SERVICES
Who Came to Georgia After the War

The following is a list of officers who held commissions during the American Revolution in the Continental Line or in the French regulars and who are known to have settled in Georgia at the end of the war. The settlement of many of these officers in Georgia can be explained in part by their military service in the state during the war, consequently the large numbers of veterans from Lee's Legion, Baylor's Dragoons, Pulaski Legion, First Maryland, Third South Carolina, and Fourth South Carolina. The inordinate number of veterans in Georgia of the Third Continental Artillery and Third Massachusetts was due to their retention in the post-war army and subsequent transfer to Georgia military posts at the Rock Landing, Point Petre, and elsewhere. Some became leading military figures in their adopted state, including Armstrong, Call, Fishbourn, Gordon, Graves, Gunn, Hampton, Long, Martin, Rudolph, Francis Smith, and Woods. These veterans played leading parts in organizing the Order of St. Tammany, several lodges of Freemasons, the Georgia Society of the Cincinnati, and several hunt clubs. Others taught music, raised thoroughbred horses, engaged in land speculation, practiced law and medicine, served as sheriffs and customs collectors, and became merchants and planters. Collectively they were among the leaders of post-war Georgia. Their presence is still felt in the state by the military units they organized, such as the Georgia Hussars (Samuel Hammond), Chatham Artillery (Edward Lloyd), Richmond Hussars (Ambrose Gordon), and Liberty Independent Troop (Michael Rudolph).

1. ANCIAUX, Nicholas, Lieutenant Quartermaster and Paymaster, Regiment Dupont (Count de Rochambeau). "The Georgia State Gazette or Independent Register," Augusta, 11 November 1786, p. 2, cols. 1-2. Died 1 September 1810 in Bulloch County, Ga.
2. ARMSTRONG, James, Captain, Lee's Legion. Heitman, 74. Colonel commanding First Georgia State Regiment (1787); Captain commanding the Hundred Horse (1793); Major, United States

Army. Resident of Augusta, Ga. Died in McIntosh County, Ga. on 28 June 1800.

3. AXSON, Samuel Jacob, Hospital Surgeons Mate, 1st South Carolina Regiment. Heitman, 79. Died in Liberty County, Ga. on 6 October 1827.
4. BALDWIN, Abraham, Chaplain, 2d Connecticut. Heitman, 82. Died 4 March 1807.
5. BEALL, Thaddeus, 2d Lieutenant, 1st Maryland Battalion of the Flying Camp. Brigade Major to General Reazin Beall, Heitman, 94. Died in Hancock County, Ga in 1815.
6. BOWEN, John, Lieutenant, 8th Virginia, died at Augusta in 1790. See "The Augusta Chronicle and Gazette of the State," 27 February 1790, p. 4, col. 1. Elegy. Late "CPT in Continental Army."
7. BOYKIN, Francis, Captain, 1st South Carolina Regiment; appointed major in Georgia Militia in 1781. Died in Baldwin County Georgia in 1821.
8. BRICE, Jacob, Captain, 1st Maryland. Heitman, 120. Major, First Brigade, Georgia Militia after war. Died at Savannah, Ga on 25 December 1788.
9. BROWN, William Stewart, Major, 1st Continental Artillery. Heitman, 127. Died on 21 September 1810 at the age of 74. "Georgian," Savannah, 1 November 1820, p. 1, col. 5. Native of Maryland
10. BULLOCK, Rice, Subaltern (Quartermaster), 15th Virginia Regiment. Heitman, 132. Member of Georgia Society of the Cincinnati
11. BURBECK, Henry, Captain, 3d Continental Artillery. Heitman, 133. Captain, Battalion of Artillery, commanding company at St. Marys River, 1790-1792.
12. BURROWES, (or Burroughs), John, Major, Spencer's Continental Regiment (New Jersey). Heitman, 135. Merchant of Georgia by 1791; died in Georgia in 1810.
13. CALL, Richard, Major, Baylor's Regiment 3d of Dragoons, Heitman, 140. Captain, Augusta Dragoons, 1787. Major, 1st. Regiment of Infantry, United States Army, commanding federal troops in Georgia, 1791-1792. Died at the Rock Landing in 1792.
14. CANTEY, James, Captain, 3d South Carolina Regiment (Rangers), died near Milledgeville, Ga. on 9 October 1817.

15. COCKE, Nathaniel, Captain, 7th Virginia. Heitman, 162. Lieutenant Colonel, Virginia Militia. Moved to Augusta, Ga. after Revolution. Died 8/18 December 1807 at Sandersville, Washington County, Ga.
16. COPP, John, Captain, 1st New York Regiment. Heitman, 171. Moved to Savannah, Ga. after the Revolution.
17. COTTINEAU, Denis L., De Gautier De Kerveguen, Captain, Continental Navy. Died at Savannah, Ga. on 29 November 1808, aged 63. "Savannah Morning News," 23 July 1905, p. 7, col. 1; 19 April 1912, p. 14, col. 4; and 22 September 1929, p. 7-C.
18. CRAWFORD, Charles, Captain 2d North Carolina Regiment. Heitman, 177. Died in Columbia County, Ga. on 22 October 1813.
19. DANIELL, Stephen Beadon, Ensign, 1st North Carolina, later transferred to the South Carolina Line. Died in Georgia about 1820.
20. DAVIS, William, Lieutenant Colonel, 5th North Carolina Regiment. Heitman, 189. Died 14 May 1818 in Wilkes County, Ga.
21. DUNCAN, David, Lieutenant, Virginia Regiment. Heitman, 206. Moved to Georgia after war.
22. DURKEE, Nathaniel, from Connecticut, commissioned Regimental Quartermaster 7th Connecticut, 1 January 1777; appointed Deputy Commissary General of Purchases, 1 October 1777. Served to 1781. Moved to Georgia after the war.
23. ELHOLM, Augustus Christian George, Lieutenant, Pulaski Legion. Heitman, 214. Adjutant General of Georgia. White, 628.
24. FIELD(S), James, Captain-Lieutenant, 4th South Carolina Regiment (Artillery). Sheriff of Chatham County.
25. FISHBOURN, Benjamin, Captain, 1st Pennsylvania, A.D.C. to General Anthony Wayne. Heitman, 227. Lieutenant Colonel, Chatham Battalion, Georgia Militia after the war. Died November 1790. Member of the Cincinnati and Freemasons.
26. FORSYTH, Robert, Major, Pulaski Legion. Heitman, 223. Murdered in 1794 by Beverly Allen. Historical Collections, NSDAR, I, 118-119.
27. FOWLE, John, 1st Lieutenant, 3d Massachussets. Heitman, 235. First Lieutenant, Battalion of Artillery. Died at the Rock Landing in Georgia about October of 1790.

28. FUHER, Charles Frederick, Captain, Virginia State Regiment.
29. GAITHER, Henry, Brevet Major, 1st Maryland. Heitman, 240. Major, 3d Sub Legion, United States Army, 1792. Lieutenant Colonel 1 October 1793. Third Infantry, 1796.
30. GINDRAT, Henry, commissioned officer under General Greene. Wounded at Battle of Eutaw. Removed from Beech Island, near Augusta, Ga., to Beaufort, S.C., where he died January/February 1801. Buried at Sisters' Ferry. Member of the Georgia House of Representatives from Effingham County, 1787-1794.
31. GORDON, Ambrose, 3d Continental Dragoons. Heitman, 253. Historical Collections, NSDAR, I, 122. Major and Colonel, Richmond County Battalion of Militia after the war. Captain, Chatham Troop of Light Horse, 1798-1804. Died at Augusta, 28 June 1804.
32. GRAVES, John, 2d Lieutenant, 8th Virginia, Major in Militia, Colonel. Commanded Georgia regiment from Wilkes County against the Creeks in 1786. White, 684-684. Heitman, 257. Lieutenant Colonel, 2d Georgia Regiment of Volunteers, 1787. Born Culpepper County, Va. Died at the age of 77 on 1 July 1824 at his plantation near Washington, Wilkes County, Ga. "Georgia Patriot," Milledgeville, 6 July 1824, p. 3, col. 3.
33. GREENE, Nathanael, Major General, Southern Department. Heitman, 260. Died in Georgia, 1786.
34. GUNN, James, Captain, 1st Continental Dragoons. Heitman, 265. Brigadier General, Georgia Militia. Died 30 July 1801.
35. HAMMOND, Samuel, Captain under the command of General Lincoln and Colonels Henderson and Malmady. Rose to rank of Colonel in State service. Appointed Major commanding 1st Battalion, 1st Regiment, Georgia Militia in 1793. Held dual command as Captain commanding the Chatham Light Dragoons. Died 22 September 1842 near Hamburg, S.C. White, 624-628.
36. HAMPTON, Henry, Captain, 6th South Carolina. Heitman, 271. Colonel, 1st Regiment of Volunteers, 1787.
37. HIWELL, John, Lieutenant, 3d Continental Artillery. Heitman, 292. Also Inspector of Musick in American Army. "Georgia Gazette," 17 February 1785, p. 4, col. 2. Lived and taught music at Savannah after the war. Died there on 15 March 1788.
38. HUGHES, Henry, Ensign, 7th Virginia Regiment. Heitman, 306.

Member of Georgia Society of the Cincinnati.
39. HUNTER, John, Surgeon, member Georgia Society of the Cincinnati.
40. JACKSON, Charles, Ensign, 3d Massachusetts. Heitman, 315. Died 25 October 1801.
41. JACKSON, Ebenezer, 2d Lieutenant, 3d Continental Artillery. Heitman, 315.
42. KENNEDY, Samuel, Captain, 2d Pennsylvania. Heitman, 329. Died 31 September 1791 in Georgia. Member of the Society of the Cincinnati and Freemasonry.
43. LLOYD, Benjamin, Lieutenant, 4th South Carolina Regiment (Artillery). Heitman, 354. Captain of Light Infantry Company, Chatham Battalion, 1785.
44. LLOYD, Edward, 1st Lieutenant, 4th South Carolina Regiment (Artillery). Heitman, 354-355. Captain, Artillery Company, Chatham Battalion, Georgia Militia, 1785-1789.
45. LONG, Nicholas, Colonel, D.Q.M.G., North Carolina. Also served as officer of dragoons, attached to the North Carolina Line. Moved to Wilkes County, Ga after the war. During the War of 1812 he was appointed Colonel commanding the 43d Regiment, U.S. Infantry, raised for the maritime defense of the Carolinas and Georgia. Was a Freemason. Died 22 August 1819 at the age of 56. "Georgia Journal," Milledgeville, 14 September 1819, p. 3, col. 3. White, 684. Heitman, 356. Surveyed the location of the state college.
46. LOWE, John Tolson, 2d Lieutenant, 1st Maryland. Heitman, 359. Moved to Franklin County, Ga. after the war.
47. McLANE, Daniel, 1st Lieutenant, 3d Continental Artillery. Heitman, 373. Captain-Lieutenant, Augusta Volunteer Company of Artillery, 1790. Lieutenant, Battalion of Artillery, U.S. Army, Beard's Bluff, Ga., 1791.
48. MARTIN, Thomas, 1st Lieutenant, 9th Virginia. Heitman, 382. Lieutenant Colonel, 1st Georgia Regiment of Volunteers, 1787. Inspector General of State Line, 1790. Captain, 1st Sub Legion, U.S. Army, 1792. Commanded unit in Georgia, 1793. Died 18 January 1819.
49. MATHEWS, George, Brevet Brigadier General, Continental Army.

Heitman, 384. Historical Collections, NSDAR, I, 130. Colonel of 9th Virginia. Brigadier General of Militia and Governor of Georgia. Died 30 August 1812.

50. MEAD, John, Ensign, 14th Virginia, Brigade Commissary of Issues. Heitman, 387. Richmond County, Ga. Deed Book F No. 6 (1796-1797), 79. Died 4 October 1798.
51. MERIWETHER, James, Lieutenant, Baylor's Regiment of Dragoons. Heitman, 390. Died 23 October 1817.
52. MONTFORD, Robert, Continental officer. See letter from Thomas Gibbons, 2 October 1789, "Georgia Gazette," Savannah. Member of Georgia Society of the Cincinnati. Captain of the East (Church) Company, Chatham Battalion, Georgia Militia, 1789-1794. Merchant of Savannah. Died on trip to Philadelphia in 1794.
53. MOSELEY, Robert, 1st Lieutenant, 8th Pennsylvania Regiment. Heitman, 404.
54. MURREN (or Murran), William, 2d Lieutenant, 2d Pennsylvania. Heitman, 408. Member of Cincinnati and Freemasonry. Died 1789.
55. NIXON, Andrew, Captain, 1st Continental Dragoons. Heitman, 414. Died at Col. Gunn's plantation on Great Ogeechee in 1790.
56. O'NEAL, Ferdinand, Captain, Lee's Legion. Heitman, 420.
57. PENDLETON, Nathaniel, Major, A.D.C. to General Nathanael Greene. Heitman, 435.
58. PENDLETON, Solomon, 1st Lieutenant, 4th New York, Heitman 435. Moved to Georgia after the war. Died in New York City on 9 January 1787.
59. PETIT, M., officer in the squadron commanded by Admiral Suffrein (French) in the East Indies during the war. Moved to Savannah afterwards. Elected Professor of Languages at the University of Georgia in 1805.
60. PIERCE, William Jr., Brevet Major, A.D.C., Southern Department. Died 10 December 1789. Heitman, 441.
61. PORTER, Moses, 2d Lieutenant, Corps of Artillery. Heitman, 447. Died 21 April 1822.
62. RAIFORD, John, Brevet 2d Lieutenant, 2d North Carolina. Died in 1812 in Jefferson County, Ga.

63. RICHARDSON, Walker, from Virginia, entered the Continental Army as a private in 1776, commissioned Lieutenant in the Foot, subsequently 2d Lieutenant, 1st Continental Artillery (4 March 1778), promoted 1st Lieutenant (18 August 1779), promoted to Captain-Lieutenant. Moved to Elbert County, Ga. after the war.
64. ROBERTS, Richard Brooke, Captain, 4th South Carolina (Artillery). A.D.C. to General Benjamin Lincoln. Heitman, 469. Captain, 2d Sub Legion, 1792. Unit commander in Georgia. 1793. Died 19 January 1797.
65. RUDOLPH (or Rudulph), Michael, Captain, Lee's Legion. Heitman, 476. Known as the "Lion of the Legion." Captain, Troop of Horse, Liberty County, Ga., in 1789. Captain, 1st U.S. Infantry, 3 June 1790, being stationed at the Rock Landing in Georgia. Appointed Major in a cavalry squadron in March of 1792 by President Washington. Appointed Adjutant and Inspector of the Army on 22 February 1793. Drowned in 1795. Born Maryland in 1753/54. Collector of Port of Sunbury, Ga. after war.
66. SANDERS, Jesse, Captain, 6th North Carolina. Subsequently Lieutenant Colonel, 1st Battalion, Richmond County Regiment, Georgia Militia, 2 February 1785. Served as such to December 1790. Commissioned Lieutenant Colonel, Columbia County Regiment, G.M., 20 January 1791.
67. SAVAGE, Joseph, Captain, 2d Continental Artillery. Heitman, 482. Captain, Battalion of Artillery, commanding at the Rock Landing on Oconee River, 1790-1792.
68. SMITH, Francis, 2d Lieutenant, 6th Virginia. Heitman, 502. Colonel in Georgia Militia after war. Served in Georgia Legislature. Died 30 August 1821.
69. SMITH, John, 2d Lieutenant, 2d Continental Artillery. Heitman, 504. Captain, 1st Regiment of Infantry, commanding at Beard's Bluff, Altamaha River, Georgia, 1790-1792.
70. SMITH, John Carroway, Brevet Major, 3d South Carolina Regiment (Rangers). Heitman, 505. Died 18 March 1800.
71. STUBBLEFIELD, Peter, 1st Lieutenant, 1st Virginia State Regiment. Heitman, 526. Commissary General of Issues for Georgia, 1787.
72. SULLIVAN, John, Captain, 4th Continental Light Dragoons. Heit-

man, 527. Leader of the Yazoo Frauds in Georgia.
73. SUMNER, Job, Major, Lieutenant Colonel, 4th Connecticut. Heitman, 527. Died October 1789 in New York.
74. TALIAFERRO, Benjamin, Brevet Major, Continental Line. Heitman, 531. Colonel, 2d Regiment Georgia State Troops, 1787. Died 3 September 1821.
75. THOMAS, Abisha, Captain, Deputy Quarter Master General, Massachusetts. Heitman, 538. Died at Darien, Ga. on 9 August 1804.
76. THOMPSON, William, 1st Lieutenant, 9th Pennsylvania. Heitman 541. Historical Collections, NSDAR, I, 119. Member of Society of Cincinnati. Died 19 March 1794.
77. TWINING, Nathaniel, 2d Lieutenant, 4th Maryland. Heitman, 553. Moved to Wilkes County, Ga.
78. VICKERS, Samuel, Surgeon.
79. WAILES, Edward Lloyd, Ensign, 6th Maryland. Heitman, 564. Died 27 January 1809 in Oglethorpe County, Ga.
80. WARD, John Peter, 1st Lieutenant, 1st South Carolina. Heitman, 568. Died 10 December 1802.
81. WATKINS, Robert, Lieutenant, 5th Virginia. Heitman, 575. Moved to Richmond County, Ga after war. Colonel. Died in Richmond County on 24 August 1805.
82. WAYNE, Anthony, Brigadier General. Heitman, 577. Died 14 December 1796. Planter of Chatham County, Ga. and political figure in state for a number of years before re-entering the active army.
83. WHITAKER, Hudson, Captain, 6th North Carolina. Moved to Baldwin County, Ga. after war. Heitman, 585. Died soon after moving to Georgia.
84. WHITE, Edward, Major, 3d Massachusetts. Heitman, 585. Moved to Savannah, Ga. Died 9 January 1812.
85. WILLIS, Francis, Captain, Grayson's Continental Regiment. Heitman, 597. Colonel, 2d Georgia Regiment of Volunteers, 1787. Moved to Wilkes County, Ga. Died 25 January 1829 after a duel.
86. WILSON, Goodwin Jr., Ensign, 14th Virginia, Brigade Commissary of Issues. Heitman, 598. Died 29 August 1799.
87. WOOD, Solomon, Lieutenant, 8th North Carolina. Heitman, 603. After war was General in Georgia Militia. Died 17 August 1815 at age 59, in Jefferson County, Ga.

THE GEORGIA STATE LINE, 1776 – 1784

1. GENERAL. The Georgia State Line was composed of those units raised on a permanent status and for a stated term of service at the expense of the state. These units were not part of the militia organization of Georgia, but were regulars in state service.

2. ORIGIN. The genesis of the Georgia State Line of the Revolution lies in the beginning of the colony itself. The predecessors of the state regulars were the provincial troops of the King. These units were full-time troops in the colony's pay. The immediate parent units of what was to become the Georgia State Line were His Majesty's Ranger Troops, two independent troops of horse-mounted infantry. Captain John Milledge commanded the First Troop. Captain James Edward Powell commanded the Second Troop. These units each numbered five officers and seventy privates. The two troops of provincials were raised in Georgia in 1759-60 and were disbanded on 31 March 1767 by order of General Thomas Gage. There were no provincial units in Georgia from that date until 1773, when the colony obtained the "Ceded Lands" from the Indians. That year a ranger company under the command of Captain Edward Barnard was formed for the new territory. Besides the captain, the unit was authorized 3 lieutenants, a quartermaster, 3 sergeants, a drummer, and 65 privates. Upon Captain Barnard's death on 6 June 1775, James Edward Powell was commissioned (12 December 1775) to replace him. A Tory, Captain Powell was forced to leave Georgia in 1777, the year following the disbanding of his unit. The enlisted men of Powell's company marched to Savannah and joined the Georgia Continentals. The Patriots are not known to have attempted to establish any permanent or regular forces for Georgia state service until January of 1776, but depended on militia troops and assistance from other states up to that time.

3. REVOLUTIONARY STATE LINE. The known units of the Georgia State Line during the Revolution were as follows:

a. GEORGIA STATE REGIMENT OF HORSE. The Georgia General Assembly authorized the raising of a state horse unit at its session of January, 1776. The first two troops had begun organization by April of 1776 as independent troops on state establishment. The First Troop, commanded by Captain William McIntosh, with Hatton Middleton as Lieutenant, was stationed in the south on the Altamaha River. The Second Troop, commanded by Captain Leonard Marbury, with Thomas Hovenden as 1st Lieutenant and Charles Middleton as 2d Lieutenant, was stationed in the "back country" of the Ceded Lands. By July two additional troops of horse had been added to state establishment. The Third Troop was commanded by Captain Benjamin Few, with Ignatius Few as 1st Lieutenant. The Fourth Troop was commanded by recently-promoted Captain Thomas Hovenden, with John Stewart as 1st Lieutenant. These four units were then constituted as the "Georgia State Regiment of Horse," as authorized by the General Assembly in January. William McIntosh was appointed to command the regiment as Lieutenant Colonel, with Leonard Marbury as Major and Anthony Norway as Adjutant. In response to a recommendation by General Charles Lee, the regiment was raised to Continental establishment with Congressional approval. With the addition of six new troops (eventually having a total of twelve troops), the regiment was thus constituted as the 4th (Georgia Continental) Regiment of Horse and eventually became known as the Georgia Light Horse.

b. MINUTE MAN BATTALIONS. In 1777 Georgia was shaken awake by the poor showing of the militia and Continentals on the Florida Expedition. The Georgia Assembly unrealistically passed a resolution to raise 15 battalions of 500 men each as minutemen, despite a report to the convention that all the effective male inhabitants in Georgia did not then amount to 2,000 men. On 3 June 1777 the Georgia House of Assembly more realistically authorized the second state corps. to be composed of two minute man battalions. The men for these battalions were to have a term of service of two years. The 1st Battalion was commanded by Colonel John Stewart, with Lieutenant Colonel Elijah Clarke as second-in-command. The 2d Battalion was commanded by Colonel Samuel Jack, with Lieutenant Colonel William Farrell as second-in-command. These two minute battalions were augmented by two companies of light horse commanded by Colonel John Coleman. Coleman's two troops were authorized and raised in May through July of 1777 and were originally to be used on the western frontiers of Georgia. The 1st Troop was commanded by Captain William Wilson. The 2d Troop was commanded by Captain William Pulliam and had an initial strength of 3 sergeants and 50 privates. As a matter of interest, it was later reported that Pullliam's Troop was in active service for 5 months and 8 days. The minute man battalions could not be properly filled and suffered heavily on the Florida Expedition of 1778. On 1 March 1778 the House of Assembly ordered the two minute battalions and the two troops of horse disbanded. This resolution was not immediately carried out. On the Florida Expedition of May-July, 1778, both minute battalions served under the command of the governor. Colonel Jack's battalion then consisted of some 500 men and 5 field pieces. Colonel Stewart's battalion then consisted of some 200 men.

c. COMPANY OF HORSE (Captain John Lamar). This troop was raised from 9 June to 22 July of 1777 for special purposes (i.e., for the security of the citizens) during the Florida Expedition of that year. The unit was authorized by the state as a Lieutenant's command. Despite this, John Lamar was commissioned as captain of the unit with the same pay and rations as a Major of Continental Light Horse. George Phillips was commissioned Lieutenant of the troop, which had twenty privates. The unit was discharged on 12 August 1777.

d. INDEPENDENT COMPANIES. The men of the two minute battalions and Coleman's light horse were ordered reorganized into five independent companies commanded by Major Jeremiah Wilder. Each company was to contain 50 men. In desperation the Assembly attempted to augment Major Wilder's command by authorizing a roving commission into East and West Florida to anyone raising a company of fifteen men or more. Major Wilder's five companies could not be fully raised, partly due to the intervening service of the minute man battalions in the Florida Expedition May—July 1778. Wilder could only accompany the expedition as an individual volunteer. He was court-martialed and broken. The five companies were disbanded in August of 1778.

e. COUNTY COMPANIES. With the failure of the Independent Companies the House of Assembly decided to place the responsibility of maintaining the state troops more squarely on the counties such units were to protect. On 31 August 1778 the Assembly authorized the raising of six companies, one for each of the six "settled" counties in Georgia, to be formed from the five disbanded independent units. Each of these county companies was to consist of 25 officers and men. The term of enlistment was to be four months. Four months later the British landed at Savannah and captured that town. They then captured the port of Sunbury to the south and the town of Augusta to the north. The Patriots fled to the back country of Wilkes County. A see-saw struggle for control of Georgia followed as the Georgia State Line collapsed.

f. GEORGIA STATE LEGION. In June of 1781 the Georgia service was revived with the authorization to Lieutenant Colonel James Jackson to raise the Georgia State Legion. The term of enlistment was one year. Jackson's Legion, as it was often called, was to consist of 100 horsemen each in three companies and 100 infantrymen each in two companies. Major Thomas Washington, formerly a Lieutenant of the 4th Georgia Continental Battalion, was second-in-command of the Legion. Jackson became Governor of Georgia after the Revolution, but Washington (real name Walsh) became a land speculator and counterfeiter. He was sentenced to death by the Court of Sessions at Charleston on 14 March 1791 and was executed on the 23d of that month. On 10 January 1782 the Legion was reduced to one troop of one Captain, two Lieutenants, one Quartermaster, one Saddler, three Sergeants, and forty Privates. After the recapture of Savannah by Patriot forces, the Georgia State Dragoons, as the troop had become known, was stationed on Skidaway Island. The unit was ordered disbanded in August of 1782, but was still in active service on Skidaway the following year.

g. FIRST BATTALION, STATE LINE. On 4 April 1782 the House of Assembly provided for a second state contingent, to consist of 200 riflemen raised in Wilkes, Richmond, and Burke Counties, which men were to be attached to the Continental command of Brigadier General Anthony Wayne. On 25 April the Assembly specified further that 150 men in five companies were to be raised, each company to consist of one Captain, one Lieutentant, and thirty Privates. Colonel Elijah Clarke was appointed to command the regiment (battalion). In reality, only three companies of 44 men (commanded respectively by Captains Richard Heard, Samuel Alexander, and Abner Bickham) could be raised. The term of service was for three months. These troops were utilized as Georgia's regular contribution to the revolutionary effort in the state until the Continental battalion for Georgia could be organized.

h. CARR'S INDEPENDENT CORPS. On 11 April 1782 a troop of 65 mounted militiamen under the command of Patrick Carr and Robert Sallett made a rapid descent upon Sunbury, killing some Tories living there. Impressed by Carr's daring, the Patriots decided to give him a permanent command. Consequently, on 21 May 1782 a third state contingent was authorized, to be commanded by Captain Patrick Carr. Named "Carr's Independent Corps," the unit was to consist of 30 men each in one troop of dragoons and one company of riflemen. The term of enlistment was for three months. The corps was to have 2 Lieutenants, 2 Captains, and a Captain-Commandant. On 25 May 1782, however, Carr was promoted to Major of the unit. His corps had originally served as a troop of volunteer rangers in Colonel James McKay's Regiment of South Carolina Militia and subsequently as an independent troop of militia dragoons in Brigadier General John Twiggs' Brigade of Georgia Militia under the provisions of a resolution by the Executive Council dated 16 October 1781. On 19 October 1782 a company of volunteer horse commanded by Captain Willoughby Barton was annexed to Carr's Legion. Georgia stood its military line down in July of 1783. The only permanent unit retained in state service was the 80-man command of Major Patrick Carr. His corps continued to act against the bands of armed marauders sweeping back and forth through Georgia. The unit was still in the field as late as September of 1784, when it was referred to as a company. It seems probable that as Jackson and Clarke operated in the country above Savannah, Carr was given the tactical area of responsibility of the southern portion of Georgia.

i. COMPANY OF ARTILLERY (Captain Thomas Lee). This company was authorized in July of 1776 as a provincial company, but in anticipation of eventual Continental service. It was raised under the command of Captain Thomas Lee on Salter's Island in the Savannah River. After constructing a battery at this location, the unit was moved to Trustee's Garden in the town of Savannah. It became popularly called "The Garden Battery." The unit was placed on Continental establishment in February of 1777 as the 3d Company, Georgia Continental Artillery.

j. COMPANY OF ARTILLERY (Captain Joseph Woodruff). This company was authorized on 13 April 1778 by the House of Assembly as a volunteer company of militia. The unit was to be considered part of the 1st Battalion (Chatham County), 1st Regiment, Georgia Militia, but on 5 August 1778 the Assembly augmented the unit to consist of one Captain, two Lieutenants, two Sergeants, two Corporals, and forty Privates. At this time the unit was effectively placed on state status and ordered to take charge of the artillery belonging to the state. It was given the secondary mission at the same time as a fire company for Savannah. The unit was placed under the command of Captain Joseph Woodruff on 26 August 1778, and an artillery park was appropriated at the yard of the Council House. Woodruff was promoted to Major shortly thereafter, in recognition of his command of the Georgia State Artillery. His company at Savannah was part of Colonel George Walton's command (Chatham County Militia) at the fall of Savannah in December of 1778, such command being destroyed by the British Light Infantry.

k. MARINES. In June of 1776 a contingent of provincial marines was raised to serve on the Georgia coast. Joseph Woodruff, who had been commissioned as Captain in the Georgia Miltia on 12 December 1775, was given command of the Marines. The unit was first stationed at Sutherland's Bluff on the southern coast of Georgia. It was subsequently ordered to duty in the Savannah River. In December of 1776 Captain Woodruff and three of his men were lured on board a schooner from St. Augustine and captured. There is no record of the Georgia Marines after this date.

l. GOVERNOR'S GUARD. This mounted command was apparently authorized and organized at Augusta in 1782, following the returning Patriots to Savannah by the end of that year. It was commanded by Major James Deveaux.

m. LANIER'S COMPANY. On 15 May 1778 Lemuel Lanier, of Burke County, was given a special commission by the Governor as commander of a company of rangers. Lanier had 20 men in his unit and served in such capacity for two and one-half months. Circumstances indicate that Lanier's company was one of those authorized with a roving commission into East Florida and West Florida.

THE GEORGIA MILITIA, 1775 – 1783

1. GENERAL. The militia forces of Georgia made up the bulk of the available fighting force in the state during the Revolution. In September of 1773 Governor James Wright reported that the number of effective militiamen in the colony amounted to 2,828. George Walton later stated that at the fall of Savannah in December of 1778 there were almost this many men in the Georgia militia. Another reliable source stated that there were under 2,000 eligible arms-bearing males in Georgia by 1777. Although many of those included in Wright's 1773 figure had been Tories and left the colony, there were almost a like number who had since settled in the Ceded Lands. The militia organization was composed of two elements. The first was the organized general militia, made up of the available eligible men (aged 16 to 60) in each general militia district. Each district was typically formed into a company of foot. Prior to July-August of 1775 company officers were appointed by the colonial governor, probably with the advice of the regimental commanders. Beginning with the purges of July-August, 1775, company officers were elected by the militiamen of their units and commissioned by the governor. The militia was the harbinger of democracy in Georgia. The various companies were organized into battalions and regiments. The 1st Regiment in 1774, for example, contained ten foot companies, one light infantry company, and one grenadier company. The second element of the Georgia Militia was that of the volunteer units. The volunteer forces are the progenitors of the present-day Georgia National Guard. The volunteers were formed out of the general militia and town guards. Since the light infantry and grenadier companies of the foot battalions were also elite units for special service, they alone were usually exempt from drafts from the general militia for the volunteer units. Membership in the volunteer units usually exempted one from dual service in the general militia. The various militia regiments and independent volunteer units together formed the militia brigade, The Georgia Brigade, the commander of which took his orders from the Governor, the commander-in-chief. The militia suffered from being poorly armed and equipped as well as having poor training and a lack of permanency in structure. As a part-time, citizen army the militia was

naturally not the well-disciplined force that was the professional army of the age. It is significant then that the militia, not the regulars, won the victories at the two best known Whig triumphs in Georgia in the war: Burke Gaol and Kettle Creek.

2. GENERAL MILITIA DURING THE REVOLUTION. The Georgia Patriots seized control of the militia establishment of the colony in July and August of 1775 by enforcing the acceptance by the officers of the "Articles of Association," the oath of allegiance to the Committee of Safety. Before the Revolution most of the larger parishes were formed into regiments, these parishes subdivided into divisions (battalions), and the divisions broken into districts (companies). The smaller parishes were typically formed as districts (companies) and/or divisions (battalions) of the larger parishes (regiments). By Section 4 of the Resolution of the Provincial Congress of 15 April 1776, provincial laws were continued in effect ("Rules and Regulations of 1776;" Georgia's first, temporary Constitution). The new government of Georgia continued to operate its militia under the terms of the Militia Act of 1773 until 6 February 1777. At this time the first permanent Constitution of Georgia was ratified. Chapter XXXV of this document specified that every county in Georgia having a minimum of 250 men was to be formed into a battalion. Additional men in the county could be formed into a second battalion, and so forth. Counties with less than 250 men were to be formed into independent companies. This same Constitution changed the parishes into counties, and the units were redesignated accordingly. The Georgia Militia was reorganized by Act of the House of Assembly dated 15 November 1778. This act allowed the creation by the Governor of volunteer troops of horse and three volunteer companies of artillery. The three artillery companies, each to have not more than 50 men, were to be individually attached to the 1st, 2d, and 3d Battalions (i.e., Regiments) of Foot Militia. This act was passed shortly before the British captured the Georgia low country, and was not completely put into effect. The Patriots in Georgia relied heavily on the militia organization. When the British captured coastal Georgia in 1778-79 and marched to Augusta, they required the inhabitants to take loyalty oaths. Eligible males were enrolled into the Tory militia. Ultimately, all remaining Georgia Militia units, except for small groups of "Refugees," either

were destroyed or surrendered. Some of the Refugee units fought their way into the Carolinas or into what is now Tennessee. These men performed valiant service in such battles as Cowpens, King's Mountain, and countless other encounters with the British and their allies. Only with the return of the Patriots in 1781 and their slow advance to the seaboard were the general militia units reconstructed. In August of 1781 the Georgia Militia was reorganized. The militia of the state was not reorganized again until the Militia Bill of 1784.

FIELD GRADE OFFICERS OF THE GEORGIA MILITIA, 1757 — 1783

1. FIRST REGIMENT. The 1st Regiment was organized in 1757, one year before the establishment of the various parishes in Georgia. Originally this regiment comprised the militia companies of the town and district of Savannah, but was eventually expanded to include the parishes of Christ Church, St. Philips, and St. Matthew's. Noble Jones was commissioned the first colonel of the regiment on 2 April 1757. Francis Harris was commissioned to replace him as colonel on 24 September 1764. Philip Delegal was commissioned to replace Harris as colonel on 10 December 1771. James Deveaux was commissioned to replace Delegal on 20 March 1775. At the same time Josiah Tattnall was commissioned lieutenant colonel and Philip Box was commissioned major of the regiment. Beginning with the early part of 1776, the regiment went through a rapid series of field officers as Savannah became the focal point in Georgia for the raising of various militia, state, and continental units calling for ranking officers. At the same time, the regiment was re-formed to contain two battalions. The 1st Battalion contained the companies of Christ Church Parish. The 2d Battalion contained the companies of St. Matthew's Parish. The disposition of St. Philip's Parish is unknown. With the arrest of Governor James Wright and the subsequent British threat to Savannah in the early part of 1776, the militia was in some confusion. Successive field grade officers were appointed to a composite corps formed at Savannah of various militia and Continental units from all over Georgia and South Carolina. This confusion was abated by the summer of 1776, by which time John Stirk was colonel of the 1st Battalion. The field officers for the 2d Battalion for 1776 are unknown. Upon the reorganization of the parishes into counties in February of 1777, Chatham County had the 1st Battalion of the regiment and Effingham County had the 2d Battalion.

   a. FIRST BATTALION (1776 — 1783).
   John Stirk, Colonel, acting as such by July 1776, appointed Lieutenant Colonel of the 3d Georgia Continental Battalion on 2 October 1776

(William Stephens, reputedly Colonel commanding in the early part of 1777)

George Walton, Colonel, commissioned 9 July 1777, captured 29 December 1778 (fall of Savannah), reappointed 21 August 1781 (reorganization of Georgia Militia), died 2 February 1804

John Martin, Colonel, acting as such by November 1881, died 1786

John Martin, Lieutenant Colonel, commissioned 24 February 1777, reappointed 21 August 1781

George Walton, Major, acting as such by 1 May 1776

Richard Wylly, Major, commissioned 24 February 1777, acting-Continental Deputy Quarter Master General by 15 December 1778, died 11 October 1801

John McCleur, Major acting as such before 6 July 1780

Charles Odingsells, Major, appointed 21 August 1781, resigned 25 July 1782, died 2 December 1810

b. SECOND BATTALION (1777 – 1783).

John Adam Treutlen, Colonel, commissioned 24 February 1777, elected Governor 8 May 1777

Philip Howell, Colonel, commissioned 26 July 1777

Andrew Elton Wells, Colonel, acting as such by 9 March 1778, died by 25 March 1778

Caleb Howell, Colonel, appointed 21 August 1781, commissioned 24 August 1781

Andrew Elton Wells, Lieutenant Colonel, commissioned 26 July 1777

Stephen Johnson, Lieutenant Colonel, appointed 21 August 1781, died 25 June 1808

Jenkin Davis, Lieutenant Colonel, acting as such by August 1782, died December 1788

Daniel Bunnell (or Bonnell), Major, commissioned 26 July 1777, Court of Inquiry held 1778, executed 18 October 1784 at Savannah

Abraham Ravot, Major, acting as such by 15 August 1778, commissioned 20 October 1778, died 14 October 1795

Daniel Howell, Major, appointed 21 August 1781, promoted to Lieutenant Colonel 15 February 1785

2. SECOND REGIMENT. The colonial militia of St. Paul's Parish formed the 2d Regiment of Militia, commanded first by Colonel David Douglass, commissioned 9 December 1757. It was commanded second by Colonel James Jackson, commissioned 19 July 1766. Lieutenant Colonel James Grierson was promoted to the command of the regiment on 15 June 1775, shortly before the Patriots took over the control of the militia establishment of the province. About the early part of 1776, the 2d Regiment was divided into two battalions, the Lower Battalion (1st Battalion) and the Upper Battalion (2d Battalion), both contained in the 2d Regiment, Georgia Militia. The identitites of the field officers are uncertain for the turbulent years of 1766-78, but seem to have been Robert Rae, Colonel for the Lower Battalion, and George Wells, Colonel of the Upper Battalion. Rae was commissioned as Lieutenant Colonel of the 3d Georgia Continental Battalion with date of rank from 5 July 1776. There were two other battalions in the 2d Regiment from 1777 to the 1779 reorganization. The 3d and 4th Battalions of Wilkes County were commanded by Colonels John Coleman and George Wells respectively. These battalions were separated from the 2d Regiment and given their own regimental status in 1779.

    a. FIRST BATTALION (LOWER BATTALION) (1779 – 1783).
       George Wells, Colonel, commissioned 15 June 1779, removed 17 August 1779 (court martialed)
       Robert Middleton, Colonel, serving as such by 1779, refugeed in 1780
       James Martin, Colonel, appointed 21 August 1781
       James McNeil, Colonel, serving as such by 12 July 1783
       George Wyche, Lieutenant Colonel, commissioned 15 June 1779
       George Downs, Lieutenant Colonel, serving as such by 4 November 1779
       James McNeil, Lieutenant Colonel, appointed 21 August 1781
       Littleberry Bostick, Lieutenant Colonel, serving as such by May 1782, suspended 27 May 1782 (Court of Inquiry)

James Martin, Major, serving as such by January of 1779

Daniel Wallicon, Major, commissioned 15 June 1779, died 6 September 1789

Humphrey Wells Jr., Major, serving as such by 4 November 1779

Archibald Beal, Major, appointed 21 August 1781

William Connell, Adjutant, appointed 26 July 1776

b. SECOND BATTALION (UPPER BATTALION) (1779 – 1783)

Benjamin Few, Colonel, serving as such by 1779, refugeed in 1780

Josiah Dunn, Colonel, appointed 21 August 1781, died in commission after 6 May 1782

Isaac Jackson, Colonel, serving as such by 1782

Greenberry (or Greenbury) Lee, Colonel, serving as such by 1784

James Ingram, Lieutenant Colonel, serving as such by January 1779, subsequently defected to the enemy

William Few, Lieutenant Colonel, commissioned 4 July 1779

Isaac Jackson, Lieutenant Colonel, appointed 21 August 1781

Josiah Winn, Major, appointed 21 August 1781

William Few, Major

3. THIRD REGIMENT. Originally organized as the Southern Division of Militia, St. John's Parish and the other parishes of the southern part of Georgia were reformed as the 3d Regiment. It was commanded successively during the colonial era by Colonels Mark Carr (commissioned about April of 1759), Kenneth Baillie (commissioned 20 April 1761), and Elisha Butler (commissioned 30 April 1766). There was only one known battalion in the regiment, the 1st Battalion, during the Revolution. It was probably anticipated that a second battalion be formed to encompass the militia companies (e.g., Captain Deiter's Company on St. Simons Island) south of St. John's Parish/Liberty County. Due to the breaking up of the southern settlements, the 2d Battalion was probably never organized. The early Revolutionary commanders of the 1st Battalion and 3d Regiment are not positively identified, but both John Baker and James Screven are named as Colonels by June of

1776. Screven was commissioned as Colonel of the 3d Georgia Continental Battalion, with date of rank from July of 1776. Baker was commissioned about April of 1777 as Colonel of the Georgia Continental Light Horse Regiment. Andrew Maybank assumed command of the St. John's militia battalion as Colonel by 20 September 1776.

    a. FIRST BATTALION (1777 – 1783).
        John Sandiford, Colonel, acting as such by 21 February 1777, commissioned 9 July 1777, resigned February 1778
        John Elliott, Colonel, elected about March 1778
        John Baker, Colonel, acting as such by June 1779, reappointed 21 August 1781 (reorganization of the Georgia Militia)
        John Elliott, Lieutenant Colonel, commissioned 9 July 1777
        John Cooper, Lieutenant Colonel, appointed 21 August 1781
        James Maxwell, Major, commissioned 9 July 1777, reappointed 21 August 1781.

    b. SECOND BATTALION.
    No evidence of formation

4. FOURTH REGIMENT. This regiment, formed from the units in St. George's Parish, was organized in 1774. John Thomas was commissioned Colonel of the regiment of 27 January of that year. Like the other regiments there were two battalions contained therein by 1776, one for the Upper Division (Halifax), commanded by Lieutenant Colonel John Jones, and one for the Lower Division (Queensborough), commanded by Lieutenant Colonel Daniel McMurphy (commissioned 3 July 1776). Field officers for the regiment beginning in 1777 were as follows:

        John Thomas, Colonel, commissioned 17 November 1777, defected to the enemy about April 1778 (arrested)
        John Jones, Colonel, serving as such by May of 1778 (captured 1780), died 16 October 1810
        Francis Pugh, Colonel, serving as such by 9 January 1779
        John Twiggs, Colonel, commissioned 23 June 1779 (to take rank from 26 January 1779, the Battle of Burke Gaol), refu-

geed in 1780, promoted to Brigadier General in 1781

John Clements, Colonel, serving as such by 1781

Asa Emanuel, Colonel, appointed 21 August 1781, resigned about November 1782

Hugh Lawson, Colonel, commissioned 23 November 1782

John Jones, Lieutenant Colonel, commissioned 17 November 1777

Lemuel Lanier, Lieutenant Colonel, serving as such by January 1779

James McKay, Lieutenant Colonel, appointed 21 August 1781, also Colonel Commandant of South Carolina Regiment of Volunteer Rangers

Francis Pugh, Major, commissioned 17 November 1777

John Twiggs, Major, serving as such by January 1779

John Clements, Major

Francis Boykin, Major, appointed 21 August 1781, formerly Captain in 1st South Carolina Continental Regiment

5. FIFTH REGIMENT. The Ceded Lands were opened to settlement in 1773. The military companies of the area were initially included in the regiment for St. Paul's Parish (2d Regiment). Upon the reorganization of the militia in 1777, Wilkes County was assigned two militia battalions, referred to as the 3d and 4th Battalions. These two battalions remained in the 2d Regiment until 1779, when they were consolidated and given the status of a full, separate regiment. Field officers from 1777 were as follows (partly conjectural):

John Coleman, Colonel (3d Battalion), acting as such by 31 July 1777, died 1778

John Dooly, Colonel (3d Battalion), acting as such by 1 June 1778

George Wells, Colonel (4th Battalion), commissioned 20 August 1777

William Candler, Lieutenant Colonel (3d Battalion)

Zachariah Lamar, Lieutenant Colonel (4th Battalion), commissioned 20 August 1777

Thomas Dooly, Major (3d Battalion), acting as such by 1777,

killed in ambush on 22 July 1777

Absolom Bedell, Major (4th Battalion), commissioned 20 August 1777

CONSOLIDATED AS REGIMENT JANUARY 1779

John Dooly, Colonel, commissioned 26 January 1779, surrendered regiment in June 1780, murdered

Elijah Clarke, Colonel, appointed 21 August 1781 (reorganization of Georgia Militia)

Elijah Clarke, Lieutenant Colonel, commissioned to rank from 26 January 1779, refugeed 1780

John Cunningham, Lieutenant Colonel, appointed 21 August 1781

Burrell (or Burwell) Smith, Major, commissioned to take from 26 January 1779, killed 8 August 1779

William Walker, Major, appointed 21 August 1781

George Dooly, Major

6. GEORGIA BRIGADE. As in Continental service, the various Georgia Militia regiments were combined from time to time to form a brigade, commonly called the Georgia Brigade. This brigade was a temporary arrangement for field service. The first such unit was the brigade formed at Savannah in the early part of 1776 and commanded by Colonel (and shortly, Brigadier General) Lachlan McIntosh. This composite brigade consisted of Georgia and South Carolina troops, regulars and militia. It was formed to meet the British naval threat to Savannah. A second brigade was formed under the command of Brigadier General James Screven for service on the Florida Expedition of 1778. It is known to have been composed in part by the militia battalions from Chatham and Liberty Counties, and included a troop of about 100 horsemen from as far away as Wilkes County. Samuel Elbert was the next officer promoted to Brigadier in the militia, retaining however his Continental commission as Colonel Commandant of the 2d Georgia Continental Battalion. His small brigade, composed principally of the remnants of the Georgia Continental Line and militia volunteers, was demolished at Briar Creek in 1779. Upon the return to Georgia in 1779

of Brigadier General Lachlan McIntosh and the Franco-American decision to attack Savannah, McIntosh was again placed in command of a composite brigade, called the 1st Georgia Brigade. As in earlier such corps, this 1779 organization included both militia and Continental troops from such states as Georgia, South Carolina, and Virginia. Included in McIntosh's brigade were the following units: 1st Virginia Continental Regiment (Colonel Richard Parker), 2d Continental Light Dragoon Regiment (Lieutenant Colonel John Jameson), Pulaski Legion (General Casimir Pulaski), Lower Richmond County Battalion (Colonel Robert Middleton), Upper Richmond County Battalion (Colonel Benjamin Few), and Wilkes County Regiment (Colonel John Dooly). Also included in the brigade was the Burke County Regiment (Colonel John Twiggs). Following the dissolution of the Southern Department after the American disasters at Savannah, Charleston, and Camden, the Patriots had to re-enter the South and reorganize their forces. In 1781 Colonel John Twiggs was promoted to Brigadier General. A return of his Georgia Brigade at Augusta on 22 November 1781 includes the following subordinate units: Georgia State Legion (Lieutenant Colonel James Jackson), Lower Richmond County Battalion (Colonel James Martin), Upper Richmond County Battalion (Colonel Josiah Dunn), and the two volunteer companies of Captain Patrick Carr (formerly of Lieutenant Colonel James McKay's Regiment of Volunteer Rangers, South Carolina Militia) and Captain William Cone.

VOLUNTEERS DURING THE REVOLUTION

1. VOLUNTEERS. Volunteer militia units were formed from time to time from the general militia organization. Typically, such volunteer units were for special purposes. The Georgia volunteers are the parent units for the present-day Georgia National Guard. There were a number of volunteer units in Georgia during the Revolution. Those which have been identified are as follows:

   a. ST. JOHN'S RIFLEMEN. On 8 January 1776, John Baker was commissioned Captain of this unit. The following month the unit served at Savannah in the action now known as "The Battle of the Riceboats." A detachment commanded by Captain Baker took part in the raid on Tybee on 1 April 1776 under the overall command of Colonel Archibald Bulloch.

   b. ST. JOHN'S RANGERS. On 9 January 1776, James Screven was commissioned captain of this unit. The following month the unit served at "The Battle of the Riceboats." It subsequently took part in the Tybee Raid under the command of Captain Screven.

   c. ARTILLERY COMPANY, SUNBURY. Captain John Hardy was commissioned on 15 May 1776 to command this volunteer company. Hardy was later commissioned as captain in the Georgia Continental Navy, commanding the galley *Congress*.

   d. VOLUNTEER COMPANY, SUNBURY. Nathaniel Saxton was commissioned Captain of this foot company on 15 May 1776. This unit, commanded at the time by Captain John Kell, was captured at the fall of Fort Morris in January of 1779.

   e. VOLUNTEER COMPANY, ST. GEORGE'S PARISH. On 15 May 1776, Peter Shand was commissioned Captain of this foot unit.

   f. VOLUNTEER COMPANY, HALIFAX, UPPER DISTRICT, ST.

GEORGE'S PARISH. This foot company was organized as early as 16 October 1775. John Griner was formally commissioned Captain of this unit on 30 August 1776.

g. AUGUSTA VOLUNTEER COMPANY. Captain Joseph Davlin commanded this foot company by 29 May 1776. Captain Robert Bonner was commissioned to replace him on 7 December 1776.

h. LIGHT HORSE VOLUNTEER TROOP. Ordered formed out of the Chatham County Battalion on 13 April 1778. It was to consist of one Captain, one Lieutenant, one Cornet, and thirty Privates. This troop had a secondary mission as the Horse Patrol for the area. Joseph Habersham was appointed as the first commander.

i. VOLUNTEER COMPANY ("THRICE BLUE COMPANY"), CHRIST CHURCH PARISH. Captain John Martin commanded this foot company as early as 1 April 1776, when a detachment commanded by Martin took part in the Tybee Raid. His Lieutenants were Joseph Farley Jr. and James Alexander. Returns for the unit carry one Captain, one Lieutenant, four Sergeants, one Fifer, one Drummer, and twenty-eight Privates.

j. VOLUNTEER COMPANY OF ARTILLERY. Authorized on 13 April 1778 by the House of Assembly as a volunteer company of militia. This unit was considered part of the 1st Battalion (Chatham County), 1st Regiment, Georgia Militia; however, on 5 August 1778 the Assembly augmented the unit to consist of one Captain, two Lieutenants, two Sergeants, two Corporals, and forty Privates. At this time the unit was effectively placed on state status and ordered to take charge of the artillery belonging to the state. It was given a secondary mission at the same time as the fire company for Savannah. The unit was placed under the command of Captain Joseph Woodruff on 26 August 1778, and an artillery park was appropriated at the yard of the Council House. Woodruff was promoted to Major shortly thereafter. His company was part of Colonel George Walton's command (Chatham County militia) at the fall of Savannah in December of 1778, such command being destroyed by the British Light Infantry.

k. INDEPENDENT COMPANY OF HORSE MILITIA (Captain Joshua Inman). Joshua Inman was commissioned Captain of this unit on 14 December 1779. The unit was authorized not more than 40 men. It was apparently raised in the vicinity of Burke County about September of 1778, since extant pay records for the unit run from 1 October 1778 to 1 January 1780.

l. VOLUNTEER COMPANY OF INFANTRY (Savannah). On 11 October 1782, Samuel Stirk was authorized to raise this unit from the different companies of militia at Savannah.

m. McKAY'S VOLUNTEER REGIMENT. Colonel James McKay (McCoy, McKoy, etc.) commanded this regiment of rangers from 1781 to 1782. Colonel McKay was a resident of Burke County, Georgia. His regiment was a South Carolina regiment of volunteer militia, but contained some Georgians. It was composed of four companies of volunteers, two being of Georgians and two of Carolinians, the entire regiment having a compliment of about 236 men when first raised (about January of 1781). These four companies served from time to time as attachments in regiments other than McKay's. The four subordinate companies were:

1. Company commanded by Captain Joseph Vince, Lieutenant Joseph Harley, and Lieutenant Jethro Wood. Raised at Steel Creek in South Carolina. Served during part of 1780 and 1781 in Colonel William Harden's South Carolina Regiment.

2. Company commanded by Captain Richard Creech. Latter attached to Colonel William Davis' South Carolina Regiment.

3. Company commanded by Captain Joshua Inman (see above). This unit's station was at Cracker's Neck, South Carolina.

4. Company commanded by Captain Patrick Carr (see above), 1st Lieutenant Michael Jones, and 2d Lieutenant Josiah

Hatcher. This company was subsequently engaged in the Sunbury Raid and was elevated to state status as "Carr's Independent Corps" the following year.

n. JAMES McKAY'S COMPANY. On 23 November 1782, Lieutenant Colonel James McKay (then holding a Georgia Militia commission as second-in-command of the Burke County militia) was commissioned by the Executive Council to raise a company of 10 or 12 men to suppress "out layers and Tories" infesting the Burke County area.

o. MILITIA DRAGOONS AND MOUNTED INFANTRY. On 16 October 1781 the Executive Council authorized the immediate raising of an unspecified number of units of militia dragoons and mounted infantrymen. Each company was to consist of a Captain, Lieutenant, and 30 Privates. The term of enlistment was for three months. The dragoons were to furnish themselves with a good horse, sword, and pistols. The infantrymen were to furnish themselves with a good horse and gun. These units were, of course, under the discipline of the militia laws. General John Twiggs, as commander of the Georgia Militia, was in overall command. The number of such units so raised is unknown, but is known to have included the volunteer companies of Captain Patrick Carr (formerly of McKay's Regiment) and Captain William Cone, attached to Twiggs' Brigade by November of that year. It may also have included a volunteer company commanded by Captain Grant, who was killed on 2 November 1781 in the assault on the British post on the Ogeechee River. It may have included as well a company of riflemen commanded by Captain James McKay (McCoy, McKoy, etc.).

p. GERMAN FUSILIERS. This company of volunteers was formed at Christ Church Parish in 1776. On 26 April of that year the following officers were commissioned for the unit: Captain Ambrose Wright, 1st Lieutenant James Gallache, 2d Lieutenant Thomas Dowl (Dowell), and 3d Lieutenant James Flint. Gallache commanded a detachment of 13 men from the company at Beaulieu, and Dowell commanded a detachment of 17 men from the company at Coffee Bluff, all on the Ogeechee River.

q. FUSILIER COMPANY (Savannah). Commanded by Captain Seth John Cuthbert, who led a detachment of the company on the Tybee Raid on 1 April 1776.

r. LIGHT INFANTRY COMPANY (Savannah). This flank company was organized at Savannah in August of 1767 under the command of Sir Patrick Houstoun. It escaped the fall of Savannah in December of 1778, but was destroyed at Briar Creek the following year. It was reorganized in 1785. In March of 1800 the unit was redesignated as the Chatham Hibernian Fusiliers, commanded by Captain Richard Dennis. Judge Thomas U.P. Charlton succeeded to command in 1802. The unit was disbanded in the latter part of 1803.

s. GRENADIER COMPANY (Savannah). This flank company was organized at Savannah in June of 1772 under the command of Captain Samuel Elbert. The unit was destroyed at the fall of Savannah in December of 1778 and not reorganized. See Gordon B. Smith, "The Georgia Grenadiers," in G.H.S. *Quarterly,* LXIV, 4 (Winter, 1980), 405-415.

t. GRENADIER COMPANY (St. Matthew's Parish). This flank company was apparently organized at Ebenezer in 1776.

2. REFUGEES. At the first Siege of Augusta in 1780, Colonel William Candler raised a volunteer regiment of "Refugees." The Refugee Regiment (known typically as "The Refugee Regiment of Richmond County") was enlisted at the direction of Colonel Elijah Clarke, as Colonel Commandant of Georgia refugee forces, on 15 September 1780 to serve "till the British are totally expelled from this state." The regiment was small, initially containing one Colonel, one Major, three Captains, five Lieutenants, and sixty-five Privates formed into three companies. As originally formed, the officers of the 1st Company were Captain Frederick Stallings, Lieutenant James Stallings, and Lieutenant Ed-

mond Martin. The officers of the 2d Company were Captain Abraham Ayres and Lieutenant Daniel Dannelly. The officers of the 3d Company were Captain Ezekiel Offutt, Lieutenant Jacob Zinn, and Lieutenant James Martin. The regiment was formally reorganized five days later with additional staff, rank and file. At this reorganization Candler's field officers were: David Robeson, Lieutenant Colonel; John Shields, Major; John McCarthy, Adjutant; and Loveless Savage, Chaplain. Robeson served until December of 1780, when Lieutenant James Martin was elected Lieutenant Colonel to replace him. Shields was killed in battle and Henry Candler replaced him as Major. Archibald Beal replaced John McCarthy as Adjutant. Candler's regiment withdrew from Georgia in September of 1780 and marched to the Nollichucky settlements in present-day Tennessee, fighting battles at King's Mountain (7 October 1780), Fishdam Ford (9 November 1780), Blackstock's Farm (20 November 1780), and Long Cane (11 December 1780) on the march. Despite the enlistment oath taken by these volunteers, the regiment was disbanded on 5 June 1781 at the final reduction of Augusta by the Patriots. Colonels Elijah Clarke and Benjamin Few also commanded refugee detachments, which were different from Candler's in that they contained South Carolina militiamen as well as Georgia refugees. Candler's regiment was the only purely refugee regiment of Georgia. Candler died in July of 1784 in present-day Columbia County, Georgia.

3. OTHER UNITS OF VOLUNTEERS. On 15 November 1778 the Militia Act authorized the creation of three volunteer militia companies of artillery, not to exceed 50 men each. These companies were to be attached to the 1st, 2d, and 3d Battalions of Foot respectively. The fall of Savannah and the events which followed prevented the raising of these units, however. This scheme was put into effect after the war with the formation of volunteer artillery companies at Savannah (Lloyd), Augusta (Howell), and Sunbury (Dollar). During the Revolution there were any number of volunteer units of varying degress of formality. There were at least two units not mentioned above which had formal commissions. Thomas Gray, an Indian halfbreed whose secret mission to East Florida in 1775 led to his arrest at St. Augustine, was given a commission on 5 March 1778 as Captain of a scouting party of Indians which had served against the Florida Scout for the previous four

months. In April of 1776 a detachment from a company of Creek volunteers served in Colonel Archibald Bulloch's command against the Tories on Tybee Island. Finally there was a Guard Company for the town of Savannah in the early days of the Revolution, such unit having been formed during the colonial period.

THE GEORGIA STATE LINE
(1787 – 1790)

In 1787 Georgia authorized the re-establishment of its regular State Line in the face of the threat of war with the Creek Indians.[1] On 31 October of that year the Georgia Assembly passed "An Act For Suppressing the Violences of the Indians."[2] This act authorized the raising of two regular state regiments with an authorized strength together of 1,500 men. Each regiment was to have 750 men divided into ten companies. The enlistees were to serve until a peace treaty with the Indians was secured. In addition to these two regular state regiments, the act also authorized the raising of two volunteer state regiments with the same table of organization as the regular ones. Field officers for the four regiments were immediately appointed as follows:[3]

FIRST REGIMENT OF STATE TROOPS
James Armstrong, Colonel
Thomas Glascock, Lieutenant Colonel
John Clark, Major

SECOND REGIMENT OF STATE TROOPS
Benjamin Taliaferro, Colonel
Francis Tennell, Lieutenant Colonel
Henry Allison, Major

FIRST REGIMENT OF VOLUNTEERS
Henry Hampton, Colonel
Thomas Martin, Lieutenant Colonel
James Fontaine, Major

SECOND REGIMENT OF VOLUNTEERS
Francis Willis, Colonel
John Graves, Lieutenant Colonel
Thomas Gilbert, Major

George Handley, Inspector General

Peter Stubblefield, Commissary General of Issues
Ignatius Geohegan, Director General of Hospitals

As during the Revolution, enlistments did not meet expectations. Consequently, on 1 February 1788 the Assembly amended the earlier act by offering additional uniform allowances to enlistees.[4] The First State Regiment, initially commanded by Col. James Armstrong,[5] was the only one of the four regiments to be raised. The initial organization of the regiment was completed in February and March of 1788. Troops of the regiment fired the artillery salute in Augusta upon Georgia's ratification of the Constitution. As companies in the regiment were completed and outfitted they were individually marched to the frontier, ultimately moving to the coast to defend the area from the Creeks.

In 1805 Robert Flournoy, a former Captain of the First Georgia, addressed a long memorial to the Assembly regarding the state's obligations to these veterans.[6] He wrote that the officers of that corps were "principally young men of little or no fortune; a great many of whom were but just settled in the state from the northward, without resources; but were anxious to defend and serve that country in which they were desirous of spending the remainder of their days..." He added that when in March of 1788 the troops were "convened" at the town of Washington, Georgia and ordered upon actual service, to their dismay they were detached in small parties and stationed along an extensive frontier. They experienced hunger, nakedness, and hard marches. He described how the soldiers were often barefooted.

In January of 1788, John Clark had been promoted to Lieutenant Colonel succeeding Armstrong in command of the regiment. His ill-starred corps is best remembered, perhaps, for a mutiny undertaken by the Sixth Company (Cpt. William Ross, 2Lt. Thomas McAvey) in 1789. This mutiny was triggered by the failure of the state to supply and provision the units, a continuing problem. On 25 March 1788 on the Oconee River near Long Bluff, Cpt. James Wood of the regiment and five of his men were driven by hunger to climb some peach trees for food. While in the trees all of the men were shot down with their own weapons and scalped by Creek warriors. The regiment is also remembered for the fatal duel between Maj. Henry Allison of the Second State Regiment and Cpt. Oliver Rock of the First State Regiment in July of 1789 on the Shoals of Ogeechee.[7]

Ironically, the regiment celebrated the document which ultimately led to ita being disbanded when it fired the salutes in 1788 for the ratification by Georgia of the Constitution. The House of Assembly decided that the terms of the Constitution necessitated the raising of a federal army, but the disbanding of the several state lines, since that document held that no state was to keep a standing army. Consequently, the Assembly passed an act on 23 December 1789 providing for the discharging of the First State Regiment.[8] On 9 February 1790 the unit held its last muster, the troops being discharged at that time.[9]

It was estimated by Governor Edward Telfair that there were 223,140 acres of land due the officers and men of the regiment for their service. The ensuing attempts to grant these men their bounty land led to much irresponsible land speculation.

The following is a list of the officers of the unit on 9 July 1789:[10]

Lieutenant Colonel John Clark
Major Joseph Ryan

Captains:	Charles Williamson	(1st Company)
	Robert Flournoy	(2d Company)
	Thomas Cole	(5th Company)
	William Horton	(3d Company)
	Samuel Beckom	(9th Company)
	William Ross	(6th Company)
	Micajah Williamson	(7th Company)
	Robert McLeod	(10th Company)
	Robert Raines	(4th Company)
	James Giles	(8th Company)
First Lieutenants:	Clem. Harrison	
	James Stewart	

         Ethelred Wood
         Sherwood Beckom
         Oliver Rock

Second Lieutenants: Edward Jones
         Dyar Frazer
         John Fow
         James Scarlett
         Gad Harrison
         Thomas McAvey
         William Walton
         Benjamin Bragg
         Joseph Dobbs
         Alexander Reeves

---

1. The beginning of the "Oconee Wars."

2. Given in full in "The Georgia State Gazette Or Independent Register," Augusta, 10 November 1787, p. 2, cols. 1-3, p. 3, cols. 1-2, and 17 November 1787, p. 1, cols. 1-3, and p. 2, col. 1.

3. Adapted from list given in "The Georgia State Gazette Or Independent Register," Augusta, 10 November 1787, p. 3, col. 3. Note the large number of former Continental officers.

4. Ibid, 23 February 1788, p. 1, cols. 1-3.

5. James Armstrong was born about 1728 in Pennsylvania. He served as a captain in the Pulaski Legion and Lee's Legion during the Revolution. He was captured at Dorchester in December of 1781 and remained a prisoner for the duration of the war. He was the only dragoon officer of Lee's Legion captured by the British. After the war he settled at Augusta and married Sarah Houstoun of Savannah on 17 February 1791. Although he accepted the command of the First State Regiment of Georgia in 1787, he turned over his unit to Clark the following year, throwing in his lot with Judge Henry Osborne, Robert Seagrove, and others in the vote fraud effort to place BG Anthony Wayne in Congress in 1791. In 1792 he organized the Second Troop of Volunteer Light Dragoons at Augusta and became its Captain. This unit became defunct later that same year. From January to December 1794 he served as Cap-

tain commanding the "Hundred Horse," a troop of horse militia in federal service in Liberty County. He subsequently re-entered the regular service of the United States Army as a Major. Armstrong died at the home of his old comrade Col. Ferdinand O'Neal in McIntosh County, Georgia on 28 June 1800.

6. "Georgia Republican & State Intelligencer," Savannah, 7 January 1805, p. 3, cols. 2-5.

7. Major Allison, formerly a distinguished officer of the Second Georgia Continental Battalion and the Georgia State Legion, was killed in the duel. "Georgia Gazette," Savannah, 23 July 1789, p. 3, col. 3.

8. "The Augusta Chronicle and Gazette of the State," Augusta, 9 January 1790, p. 1, cols. 1-3.

9. Addresses of Edward Telfair and Seaborn Jones, "Georgia Gazette," Savannah, 17 June 1790, p. 2, cols. 2-3 and p. 3, col. 1.

10. *Georgia Military Affairs,* I (1775-1793), 278 (adapted).

The following photographs are representative of the documents from which this book was compiled.

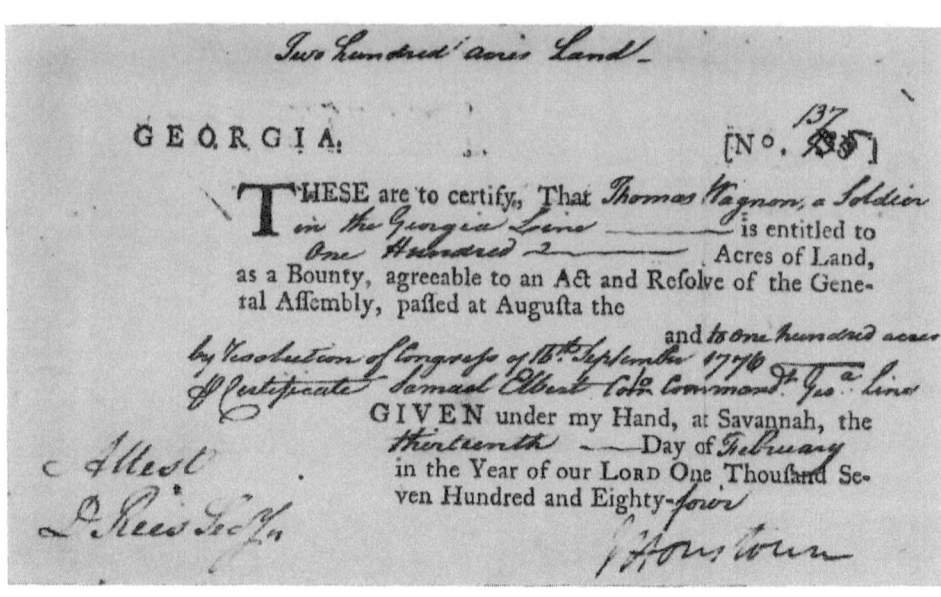

Certificate showing Thomas Wagnon was a Soldier in the Georgia Line, dated February 13, 1784. Document signed by Governor John Houstoun and countersigned by his Executive Secretary, David Rees.

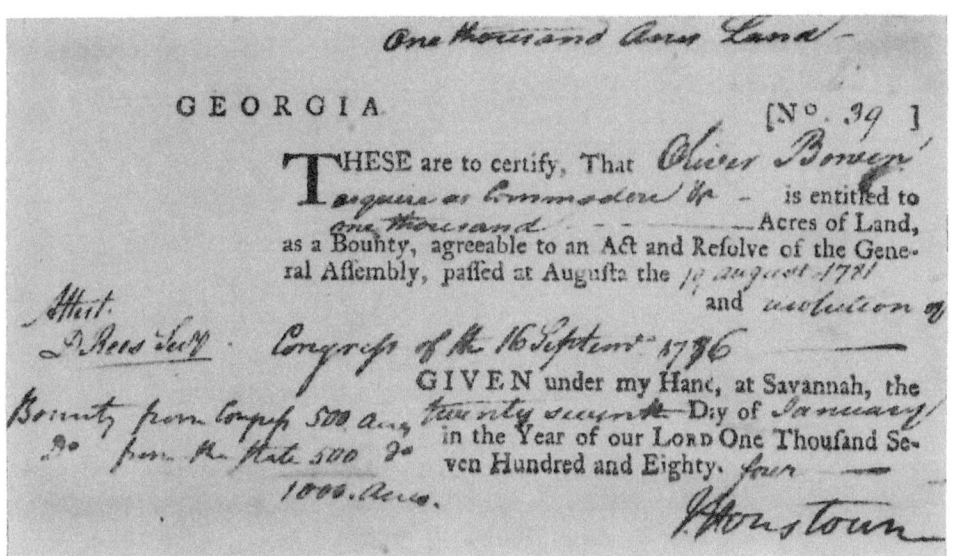

Document, dated January 27, 1784, showing Oliver Bowen was eligible for bounty land, Bowen was commander of and a commodore in the Georgia Navy. Certificate signed by Governor John Houstoun.

STATE OF GEORGIA.

THIS is to certify, That *James Taylor* was *Commissioned* to serve as a *Captain* in the ——— Battalion of Minute-Men, raised for the Defence of this State, by Resolve of Assembly, passed the 3d June, 1777; and that the said *James Taylor* ——— was not, at the Time of his *Commission* ——— an Inhabitant of this State, nor had he resided in any Part thereof for *Twelve* Months preceeding his *Commission* And further, That he was in Service at the Time the said Battalion was reduced by a subsequent Resolve of March 1st, 1778.

Given under my Hand, at *Augusta* this 22_Day of *April* — 1784.

Sam. Jack Col

Voucher, indicating that James Taylor was a Captain in Georgia's Battalion of Minute Men. This document, dated April 22, 1784, was signed by his commanding officer, Colonel Samuel Jack.

> **STATE OF GEORGIA.**
>
> THESE are to certify, That *Isham Thompson* was an Inhabitant of this State prior to the Reduction thereof by the British Arms, and was a Refugee from the same, during which Time he cheerfully did his Duty as a *Soldier* and Friend to this and the United States.
>
> Given under my Hand, this *Second* Day of *Feby 1784*
>
> By his Order
> *H Freeman*
> *Elijah Clarke Col*

Voucher, dated February 2, 1784, showing Isham Thompson was a Refugee from Georgia. This document was signed by Holoman Freeman, aid to Colonel Elijah Clarke (the latter was illiterate and could not sign his name).

GEORGIA.　　　　　　Washington,　　　　February, 1790.

THE bearer _____ _____ in the ____ regiment of State troops, and in the _____ company, commanded by _____ having faithfully served the time required by law, is hereby difcharged; and is entitled to a bounty of _____ acres of land, as recognized by "An Act for making compenfation to the troops in the fervice of this ftate," &c. paffed at Augufta the 24th December, 1789, and fhall receive the fame when fpecial appropriations are made by law.

Voucher showing Private Joseph Terrill as having served in the First Regiment of State Troops. This document, dated February 9, 1790, is signed by John Clarke, Lieut. Colonel Commanding; James Meriwether, Auditor, Pro. Tem.; and Thomas Martin, Inspector General of the State Troops.

> GEORGIA.   COMPTROLLER GENERAL'S OFFICE
> No. 121.   LOUISVILLE, 30th April 1799
>
> [CHECQUE AUTHENTICATED CERTIFICATE.]
>
> This will certify, that the original authenticated Certificate, in the words following, to wit:
>
> "GEORGIA. Washington 9th Feb'y 1790
>
> "The Bearer Lieut Edward Jones in the First Regiment of State Troops, and in the First Company, commanded by Coll Williamson having faithfully served the time required by law, is hereby discharged, and is entitled to a Bounty of seven hundred & fifty Acres of land, as recognized by "An Act for making compensation to the Troops in the service of this State, &c. passed at Augusta the 24th December, 1789, and shall receive the same when special appropriations are made by law."
>
> [signatures]
>
> has been deposited and filed in my Office, agreeably to an Act of the General Assembly, entitled, "An Act for calling in the outstanding evidences of Debts due from this State, and for issuing new ones in lieu thereof, under proper Checques and restrictions," passed the 2nd of February, 1798; and that the holder hereof is entitled to the Bounty of seven hundred and fifty Acres of Land, in the original Certificate expressed.
>
> [signature]

Certificate of Lieut. Edward Jones, dated April 30, 1799, indicating he was eligible for bounty land. Document signed by James Meriwether, Comptroller General.

www.ingramcontent.com/pod-product-compliance
Lightning Source LLC
Chambersburg PA
CBHW030553080526
44585CB00012B/359